WARRIOR'S MINDSET

PETER ADEGBIE

Warrior's Mindset

Goldenpot Publication
Copyright © 2015 by Peter Adegbie

ISBN: 978-1-911109-00-6

Published by Goldenpot Publication. All rights reserved.

Cover Design and Page Layout
Kenteba Kreations
www.kentebakreations.com

Published in the United Kingdom by GOLDEN POT MEDIA.
All rights reserved. No portion of this book may be used without the written permission of the publisher, with the exception of brief excerpts in magazines, articles, reviews etc.
For further information or permission, address:
Golden Pot Media
MICC Cornhill Road
SR5 1RU
Website:Goldenpotmedia.com
E-mail:pastorpeter@goldenpot.com
:adegbiepk@yahoo.com

All scripture quotations are from the King James Version of the Bible except otherwise stated.

Contents

Foreword 7

Introduction 9

CHAPTER ONE
Who Is A Warrior? 21

CHAPTER TWO
Warriors Contend 37

CHAPTER THREE
Warriors Renew Their Mind 49

CHAPTER FOUR
How To Exercise Your Spirit And Prevail   57

CHAPTER FIVE
Warriors Understand Spiritual Timing   71

CHAPTER SIX
Warriors Fight The Fight Of Faith   87

CHAPTER SEVEN
Warriors Refuse To Fear   109

POST SCRIPT
March Forward In Faith Like The Warrior You Are   123

Foreword

It is with great pleasure that I can endorse this book written by Dr Adegbie. I have had the pleasure to listen to his ministry over a number of years and have been impressed by his depth of insight and teaching into the practical aspects of the Christian's walk.

One of the main motto's of his church, and which is emphasised on numerous occasions, is to make 'agents of change'. This he does in different ways, one of which being, every Christian should be a spiritual warrior. There is no room for complacency and letting others do the work. We are all involved in this battle to live holy, sanctified lives and make disciples as the Lord Jesus instructed us to do. It is only achieved by being a warrior and the battle is tough, but we have the victory!

This is a very practical book and outlines for the believer the way the enemy attacks and what can be done to come against him.

I have no hesitation in endorsing this book and praying that it will be extensively used, as the contents are important for all believers. This applies whether a person is newly converted or has been on the Christian walk for many years. There is something here for everyone, which will bring blessing, encouragement and effectiveness in their Christian walk.

Dr Raymond Dennis

Introduction

Some time ago, The Lord said to me, "bring my people into a mindset of victory, until everyone has the boldness of a lion and the skills of a warrior."

The world as we know it today is an arena of warfare, whether we are conscious of it or we deliberately ignore it does not stop the fact. Creation itself attests to the reality of warfare in this realm of existence; the very process of conception as millions of spermatozoa race towards an egg is a race for life where often, only one strikes lucky. The process of embryonic development that follows is also subject to many challenges but at full gestation, when the baby is now ready to leave the warmth of the womb for the harsh realities of the world, we see the struggle repeat itself. The baby must cooperate with the mother's push and fight through the birth canal to burst forth into the harsh reality of the world outside the womb taking its first gasps of air and screaming, proclaiming as it were that it has entered a new dimension where only those who know how to fight get ahead, where only those who push progress, and where only those who keep going eventually get somewhere.

The scriptures from the Book of Revelation by the Apostle John provide the stimuli for meditation on this subject and they deeply demonstrate this principle and are the foundation for a series of teachings and discussions in church that has resulted in this book.

"He who has an ear let him hear what the Spirit says to the churches. To him who overcomes I will give to eat from the tree of life, which is in the midst of the Paradise of God."
Revelation 2:7 NKJV

"He who has an ear let him hear what the Spirit says to the churches. He who overcomes shall not be hurt by the second death."
Revelation 2:11 NKJV

"He who has an ear, let him hear what the Spirit says to the churches. To him who overcomes I will give some of the hidden manna to eat. And I will give him a white stone, and on the stone a new name written which no one knows except him who receives it."
Revelation 2:17 NKJV

"And he who overcomes, and keeps My works until the end, to him I will give power over the nations"
Revelation 2:26 NKJV

"He who overcomes shall be clothed in white garments, and I will not blot out his name from the Book of Life; but I will confess his name before My Father and before His angels."
Revelation 3:5 NKJV

> "He who overcomes, I will make him a pillar in the temple of My God, and he shall go out no more. I will write on him the name of My God and the name of the city of My God, the New Jerusalem, which comes down out of heaven from My God. And I will write on him My new name."
> Revelation 3:12 NKJV

> "To him who overcomes I will grant to sit with Me on My throne, as I also overcame and sat down with My Father on His throne."
> Revelation 3:21 NKJV

> "He who overcomes shall inherit all things, and I will be his God and he shall be My son.
> Revelation 21:7 NKJV

The verb 'overcome' is used over and over again in the above scriptures. To overcome implies engaging in an exercise or behavior that causes you to gain control over something. It means making an effort that results in gaining something desired. To 'overcome' has other synonyms and these include, to subdue, to vanquish, to conquer, to prevail and be victorious, to vanquish an opponent or make him less or worse, to defeat or disband an enemy or to cross over into enemy territory and go beyond it. The overcoming life is portrayed in these passages not only as a requirement but an achievable attainment that will enable Christians on earth to enjoy the privileges of a heavenly life.

There is consequently a heavenly life that is triumphant in its ability to overcome all challenges, and this overcoming life is available to everyone who is born of God. There is no one in Christ who is excluded or disadvantaged from participating in and enjoying the privileges of this heavenly life on earth. The implications of these passages are quite profound; that a Christian life is expected to be an overcoming life not just in theory or doctrine but also in every practical facet of life. A believer's life of faith takes its source from God. When Christ is received into the heart and life, something incredible takes place, there is impartation of the heavenly resurrected life from Christ such that whoever receives this life of God through Christ receives the same supernatural ability to conquer circumstances in the natural realm of existence as Christ did. This is because not only is God supreme, He also rules and reigns over all situations. A life in Christ as 'the righteousness of God' should therefore be one of continuous victory when it has an unshakeable root in faith.

Faith simply believes what God says and acts on it. There is an awesome potential power in this truth of Christ in us but we must release the power by believing and acting on what we believe. The acting out or practice of what we believe is enhanced by the practice of meditation in our mind, which must go on until what we dwell on within, becomes our behaviour without. There is a mindset therefore, a default mode of our senses where we believe that faith in God and what He has said can enable us to overcome whatever obstacles life may put before us. Apostle John expresses it this way:

> *"For everyone born of God overcomes the world. This is the victory that has overcome the world, even our faith."*
> *1 John 5:4 NIV*

> *"For every child of God overcomes the world; and the victorious principle which has overcome the world is our faith." 1 John 5:4 WMT*

> *"Whatsoever takes its origin from God must need triumph over the world."*
> *1 John 5:4 (James Knox)*

This is the victorious principle called faith that ensures that whoever takes origin from God must triumph over the challenges and situations of the world. So what does it take to overcome or how do we overcome?

Let's start from the beginning. The book of beginnings is Genesis and from there we can understand God's original intent for mankind. What He told Adam and Eve originally still remains His heart's desire for every man and woman, God said, 'have dominion.' Man was made in the image and likeness of God and was destined or wired up to dominate and subdue the natural world simply because his own existence was governed by something beyond the natural - the spirit realm.

"Then God said, "Let Us make man in Our image, according to Our likeness; let them have dominion over the fish of the sea, over the birds of the air, and over the cattle, over all the earth and over every creeping thing that creeps on the earth."
Genesis 1:26 NKJV

The original intention of God was for you and I to exercise the dominion of our spiritual resources and godlike nature over everything in the physical realm. Adam and Eve lost their access to this realm through carnality because they trusted more in the mental and physical realm than the spiritual. Since that costly mistake, man has been engaged in a battle of wits with the devil the father of lies and deception. Therefore, in order to successfully engage with and develop a mind that habitually triumphs over situations and challenges, you must firstly believe that God will not allow any situation to come into your life that you are not equipped and empowered already to subdue. Please don't be deceived, God is not wicked, if it is rough or tough it is because there are some things rougher and tougher inside you that are able to deal with the situation.

Until you can engage with what God has subtly been growing in you, you never realize the possibilities of your potential. You are never to give up until you win, because faith in God's love for you stirs you to accept and believe it is your destiny to win according to God's word. He expresses through the prophet Jeremiah that,

> "For I know the thoughts that I think toward you, saith the LORD, thoughts of peace, and not of evil, to give you an expected end."
> Jeremiah 29:11 NKJV

The Holy Spirit is given to you as your incredible helper who helps you in this inward godly motivation to succeed, to dominate and subdue; He whose help can make you prevail and conquer is already inside you. All you will ever need is already within.

This is how the mind of heavenly citizen's should work, from within them, those who triumph all the time are able to develop a fearless courage that grows stronger and stronger as faith develops through an understanding of the complete redemptive work of Jesus Christ. The assurance and infallibility of God's word and promises to those who believe is what stirs up a worldview and mindset within that looks at challenges and difficulties and roars back with a courageous heart until victory is won.

> "You are of God, little children, and have overcome them, because He who is in you is greater than he who is in the world."
> 1 John 4:4 NKJV

Christ in you is what becomes manifest as an overcoming

mentality that enables the believer to live a warrior's way of life, to have a default mindset that will not accept defeat. I think this is why the injunction to overcome is repeated so many times at the beginning and at the end of the book of Revelation. There is already someone inside you who cannot be defeated, who is greater than whatever challenge or opposition you may face in this world. Simply believe that because you are born of God, you have been empowered to overcome. Certain children of noble birth just assume and behave success because they have no expectation of failure. I remember when the Prince of Wales was interviewed and was asked how it felt to be heir to the throne of England, his answer was quite insightful and instructive, "how am I supposed to feel" he responded almost incredulously, "I am born to be king."

This is the same degree of belief and certainty everyone who is an heir of salvation and joint heir with Jesus Christ should demonstrate. Now, the decision to overcome or to exercise this privilege conferred on the believer depends on the believer accepting personal responsibility. The determination to overcome and fulfill the potential of what we can be is a state of mind that needs to be cultivated. This is why I have written this book. I believe God wants every Christian believer to become empowered and to overcome in every situation.

'To him that overcomes' is an injunction that implies, each one must take on the responsibility and accept the grace already deposited in him or her to overcome. It also implies there is a reward for accepting that responsibility, "to him will I give to eat of the tree of life, which is in the midst of the paradise of God."

This is repeated eight times. The purpose of repetition is to emphasize importance. I think it is crucial to God that you and I walk in victory and overcome in a way to fulfill life and purpose. It is also important to know that each one has a responsibility to develop a mind that thinks victory and not defeat. Reading through the text I find it actually frightening. if not intimidating, the implication that it is possible to have this power to overcome within and still be defeated simply because we fail to use it! That the act of refusing to exercise the right, the privilege and power to overcome, could lead to you being blotted out of the book of life!

> *"He who overcomes shall be clothed in white garments, and I will not blot out his name from the Book of Life; but I will confess his name before My Father and before His angels."*
> *Revelation 3:5 NKJV*

This is a call to sit up, don't stagnate under assumptions; it is quite possible to have the power to overcome and not use it because of ignorance, rebellion, intimidation or fear. Whatever excuses you may have, when you refuse to exercise your faith, you will lose your right to overcome. To think that those who refuse to overcome could be struck off the book of life should fire you up to break the yoke of procrastination in your life and spur you to action. It is time to become mindful of this fact; our salvation in Christ goes beyond saying the sinner's prayer and sitting in a church pew, it is a life that you live every day, on the street, at work and at home. It is living daily in the power and guidance of the Holy Spirit. Paul admonishes the Philippians and commands them to work out their salvation with fear and trembling. A treasure of great worth has been placed in your hands you cannot afford to drop the ball; you cannot afford to lose in the race of life. The stakes of heaven are high, the help of the Holy Ghost is near, and the name and blood of Jesus Christ are readily available weapons, why should you fail?

You must be determined to overcome, knowing that God has made provision for you to do so. I pray right now in the name of Jesus Christ, the name above all names, the name to which every knee must bow and every tongue confess and I decree that whatever has withstood you in life until now will bow to you; that the living word of God will penetrate your heart and mind and set you on your feet. That the spirit in God's word that has the ability to pierce through and divide between soul and spirit will connect you with the perfect will of God for your life. There is a word or phrase in season that will fire up your spirit man and transform you as you read this book so that you are never the same again. I pray that from within this book, a word will proceed from God's heart into yours, that the Spirit of the living God will enlighten your spirit until you declare, "Wow! Satan, not again, you can't cheat me anymore".

Everyone that ever had a breakthrough in life had to fight and contend for his or her spiritual inheritance. It takes insight, it takes understanding and it takes determination to know and appropriate a certain behavior that demonstrates to your opposition that you believe God has already accomplished the battle for you.

Apostle Paul expresses it this way,

"and not in any way terrified by your adversaries, which is to them a proof of perdition, but to you of salvation, and that from God."
Philippians 1:28 NKJV

In the Pauline epistles, we find the apostle passionately praying again and again for believers to receive wisdom and understanding in the knowledge of God's will and be empowered to walk in all their inheritance in God.

It is time to understand how to stand as a warrior who overcomes. It is time to understand that the opposition, he who causes the difficulties in our lives, is already overcome. As long as you don't know what belongs to you, it is as useless as it not belonging to you in the first place. But when you understand what belongs to you and you sit down passively and do nothing about it, it is an abuse of that knowledge. There is no one who ever amounted to anything who did not contend for something.

> *"Set out now and cross the Arnon Gorge. See, I have given into your hand Sihon the Amorite, king of Heshbon, and his country. Begin to take possession of it and engage him in battle."*
> *Deuteronomy 2:24 NIV*

> *"Get ready and set out for the Wadi Arnon. Look! I've given into your control Sihon the Amorite, king of Heshbon, along with his land. Prepare to take possession by provoking him to war."*
> *Deuteronomy 2:24 ISV*

The use of words here is interesting, even though God said that He has 'given' this territory to the Israelites, they were to take possession of this inheritance by engaging with the opposition in battle, the International Standard Version says by 'provoking' the enemy to war. Though God gave the Israelites a guarantee that the land should be their own, yet they must contend with the enemy and provoke the opposition to get at what God has promised. Whatever God gives you; you must venture to get. This implies that there are certain things that belong to you but may never become yours until you fight for it. You must learn to think like a warrior.

"This day I will begin to put the dread and fear of you upon the nations under the whole heaven, who shall hear the report of you, and shall tremble and be in anguish because of you."
Deuteronomy 2:25 NKJV

God has already put fear and dreads of you in the heart of your enemy so do not fear. But many times even though the roar of the Lion of the tribe of Judah is within us, we continue to run helter-skelter from a fake lion that has no teeth. God wants you to stand your ground and roar back, "No! Enough." Until you resist the enemy you never know just how weak he is. Resist and he will flee from you. He who has put dread and fear inside the devil is called Jesus Christ, and if you are saved, you are His perfect image. Christ who routed Satan, who made an open show of him, who took back power and authority from the devil now lives in you. There is a fear and dread of you in the realms of darkness because light dwells within you and that light shines in darkness and darkness comprehends it not. The revelation and light of God's word inside you is one that darkness cannot handle. Wow! It is time to begin to understand that there is secure strength inside you.

1

WHO IS A WARRIOR?

A general definition of a warrior is, a skilled combatant in the art of warfare, a disciplined fighter who demonstrates great courage and vigour in pursuit of what he or she believes in. This is the portrait of who God wants you to be in a spiritual sense. God wants you to be courageous and vigorous in the pursuit of what you find and believe in His word. If you believe it is possible to live a holy life and walk in the power and anointing of the Holy Spirit, then you will receive grace to do so. If you believe that signs and wonders will follow you and that the mighty gifts of the Holy Spirit will manifest through you then you will experience what you expect. This principle of becoming what you see or receiving what you can see was demonstrated in the life of Abram after Lot departed from him, God commanded him to lift up his eyes.

> *"And the LORD said to Abram, after Lot had separated from him: "Lift your eyes now and look from the place where you are— northward, southward, eastward, and westward;"*
> *Genesis 13:14 NKJV*

What you cannot see, you cannot take hold of. Every conquest begins with vision, it is vision that creates an expectation and often, it is only what you expect that you eventually experience. A warrior in Christ not only believes in the reality of the supernatural but will also be diligent in the pursuit of self-discipline and self-discovery in order to experience that supernatural reality that enables him or her to become a blessing to others.

The word 'warrior' is derived from Anglo-French origin and it means to wage war. The concept of being a 'warrior' has as much fascination today as it did in ancient and medieval times when the noble Knights of Europe, the Samurai class of Japan, Amazonians of Greek mythology, Khalsa and Kshatriya of ancient India and others that we would refer to today as Special Forces, served their kings and kingdoms and were revered in their society for courage and bravery. Currently, the word 'warrior' is still used as choice branding for various things from military navy ships to motorcycles because it continues to communicate to us an image of strength, reliability and invincibility.

In contemporary culture, several films have been made and songs performed on this common perception of the warrior. I remember in particular a film in the eighties about a New York street gang called 'The Warriors'. They were set up by another gang and wrongly accused of killing the leader of a rival gang who outnumbered them massively. This gang nicknamed 'Warriors' including a girl had to do battle throughout the night from Coney Island to Manhattan and the Bronx fighting for their lives in the subculture and mean inner city jungle of the survival of the fittest. They demonstrated the true meaning of loyalty to one another and resilience in face of overwhelming opposition.

Throughout human history and even today, the myth continues to be perpetuated of this class of beings who are renowned for discipline, bravery, strength and skill because there is something within us all that crave the heroic. Cult heroes are a constant reminder of the desire in each of us for a conquering faith that wins, conviction that survives the harshest conditions and succeeds in making it through to the end. We buy best sellers and pay to watch box office hits because of characters in movies that exemplify qualities of extreme courage, dogged perseverance and resilience in the face of hardship or danger.

Warriors have been called different names by different cultures but the values they share have always and continue to be unique and universal. In all the different types and across the centuries, certain characteristics identify and separate warriors from common men and women. They earn respect because they subject themselves to strict codes of conduct. They often go through stringent initiation rites just to ensure that their ranks were not contaminated. These ethical or honour codes were established to ensure that those called to be warriors had value for the importance of honour and that from an understanding of honour, they could demonstrate faith, loyalty and courage. These are the unique qualities we explore in this book. What does it take to be a spiritual warrior and how can one live as a successful warrior in the 21st century?

Self Discovery

The warrior's journey of becoming beneficial to others begins with self-discovery. Self-discovery is what gives you the confidence that you are not exempt from the grace of God and that God's virtue can flow through your life; that the gifts of the Holy Spirit can pour out from you like an unending river of life bringing eternal life to multitudes. Believing in Jesus and receiving Him as Lord and Saviour gives you the unique access of making the most of your life. Yes, Christ came to give abundant life to everyone that receives Him but the extent to which you can recover and enjoy the abundance that has been prepared for you depends on the amount of self-discovery you can make.

"For to this end I also wrote, that I might put you to the test, whether you are obedient in all things. Now whom you forgive anything, I also forgive. For if indeed I have forgiven anything, I have forgiven that one for your sakes in the presence of Christ, lest Satan should take advantage of us; for we are not ignorant of his devices. Furthermore, when I came to Troas to preach Christ's gospel, and a door was opened to me by the Lord,"
2 Corinthians 2:9-12 NKJV

The greatest treasure you need to discover is within you. Jesus declared that the glory the Father gave to Him has now been passed on to each person that receives Him. So what are you waiting for? Glory represents the full manifestation or full weight and expression of a thing. All things continually work together for good for those who love God and are called according to His purpose. There is a purpose in the heart of God for you, something God marked out from the very beginning, God marked you out as His own, to be made into the likeness of His son and to be a joint heir with

Christ of the grace of life. So, when the time came, He called you, declared you righteous and began to process you for a glorious existence. You are marked out and destined for a glorious life. You belong to a company of warriors who are destined to win because of the victory Christ already won. You have been given grace and opportunity to manifest and become all you can be on earth. Jesus can therefore be rightly regarded as the archetype of this new warrior class; although some people struggle to accept His identity and who He claims to be, one thing is profoundly clear, Jesus knew exactly who he was. He said,

> *"If anyone serves Me, let him follow Me; and where I am, there My servant will be also. If anyone serves Me, him My Father will honour."*
> *John 12:26 NKJV*

If you are to truly follow Jesus the author and finisher of your faith and become everything God designed you to be, you must know who you are. Jesus primarily wants you to find yourself. Have you ever considered the fact that your uniqueness is connected to your life assignment?

Finding fulfillment in your assignment of life begins with finding your identity and becoming self aware; it is your self-awareness that will provoke your God vision. If you are not clear about your identity, you will not know what to fight for and what to pursue. You may even end up substituting habits and reflections of the social mirror, contemporary culture or environmental influences for your identity. You have to know who you are. The warrior's fight begins with self-awareness that leads to self-acceptance. When a warrior identifies what is truly and deeply important then the journey of focus can begin. Self-acceptance is what gives the strength required to overcome opposition and stand-alone if needs be. Self-acceptance makes you accept your uniqueness and the reality that everybody cannot like you or be like you. In fact, what makes someone to love you might make somebody else hate you. Who you are, your gift and your vision will attract certain types of opposition. But warriors, through the power of self-awareness understand that the rise of opposition is merely the proof of a strong position and that those who become too mindful of opposition will soon lose their strong position. Opposition to the warrior is what helps to sharpen the skills they need to excel in warfare. When your sense of identity is clear and you begin to understand your assignment, it will help you to develop the power of focus.

Self-awareness helps you to distinguish between wishful thinking and what you are actually good and skilled at doing. It provokes understanding of your motivation and what truly gives you satisfaction and it also helps to define set values and priorities for your life. The Bible says, "As a man thinks in his heart so is he" I will venture to add that "As a man thinks in his heart so he sees," your self-awareness dictates the lens from which you view your world. If you don't begin to identify your worth and be aware of your uniqueness you may never generate enough strong desire to fulfill God's purpose for your life.

Focus

> *"The lamp of the body is the eye. If therefore your eye is good, your whole body will be full of light."*
> *Matthew 6:22 NKJV*

Self-awareness and acceptance is what leads to focus. You

must have a strong focus to make the most of life. Jesus had a clear and well-defined purpose that He focused on. If you don't begin to identify clear goals and objectives you may get frustrated when you find that hard work is not giving you comparative or commensurate results. A warrior trains both body and mind in order to develop and maintain mental focus because she or he understands that no success can be achieved with an unfocused mind. The development of the essential skills of warfare required to competently deal with the issues of life depends on the mastery of focus. Someone once remarked that focus is life. You can't succeed without focus; you can't lead if you lose focus easily because you might make great mistakes that will put other people's lives at risk. The warrior understands that right focus may be the difference between life and death and so refuses to lose focus. Mike Murdock says, "Men fail not because they lack resources or skill but because they lose focus."

> *"You will keep him in perfect peace,*
> *Whose mind is stayed on You,*
> *Because he trusts in You."*
> *Isaiah 26:3 NKJV*

Focus creates peace, brings great concord, harmony and vigour into our lives. God loves and honours focus. When you have focus and refuse to be distracted, there is no opposition that can stop you. Satan's power is built around deception and distraction; the ability to make you lose focus is his greatest strategy. He knows that once you are out of focus, you can no longer see the way clearly and can be easily delayed or even stagnated. To be a warrior you must refuse to lose focus. When your mind is stayed on God there is an inner peace released in you. People around you may think you are going through a tough time but because your mind is stayed on God, you are at peace. In spite of challenges, you are so much in touch with God that your joy is not tampered with or reduced in any way. Your strength is renewed every morning; you remain on fire, transported on the wings of the spirit. You are no more walking in your strength but carried on the wings of the eagle. The eagle doesn't exert so much of its own strength; it perches on a mountain ledge and sniffs the air to know where the wind is blowing before launching out with spread wings so the wind carries it on. It doesn't struggle as other birds' do it just soars. This is how God wants you to soar on the wings of the Holy Spirit. When your mind is focused on God, confident and trusting, you will hear His voice and He will lead you. Lack of focus is what often hinders divine direction.

"The wind blows where it wishes, and you hear the sound of it, but cannot tell where it comes from and where it goes. So is everyone who is born of the Spirit." John 3:8 NKJV

When you are a focused warrior, other people around you will surely hear the sound and see the signs and wonders happening in your life but nobody will be able to discern how they are happening because you are operating in the realm of the supernatural beyond the natural, riding high on the wings of the eagle. This is the warrior's trademark.

> *"If any of you lacks wisdom, let him ask of God, who gives to all liberally and without reproach, and it will be given to him. But let him ask in faith, with no doubting, for he who doubts is like a wave of the sea driven and tossed by the wind. For let not that man suppose that he will receive anything from the Lord; he is a double-minded man, unstable in all his ways."*
> *James 1:5-8 NKJV*

God hates indecisiveness and lack of focus.

Case Study: Samson

The book of Judges covers a 200-year history between the death of Joshua and the coronation of Saul the first king of Israel. At this crucial time we learn of several judges who ruled Israel, perhaps the most popular being Deborah, Gideon and Samson. Samson who is mentioned in Hebrews 11 as one of the heroes of faith, judged Israel for about twenty years. He came on the scene when Israel had been under Philistine oppression for forty years. Israel had continued to revolve in and out of a continuous cycle of sin, judgment and repentance. Like many people today, the nation only turned back to God when something hit them that they could not handle. Samson was from the tribe of Dan; this was the last tribe to settle in the Promised Land and remarkably the tribe chosen for a visitation by God. There are many crucial salient points we must learn from the story of Samson. The most important lesson perhaps is that God is always the source of vision for your life and therefore it is vitally important to stay focused on God. We are first introduced to Samson's parents in Judges 13 as the recipient of a heavenly visitation about a child they would have. The instructions given to Samson's parents by the angel were given to help Samson accomplish a level of purity that would help him develop a relationship with God when he was born. This was primarily so he could stay focused on his assignment.

A pure heart will always help you to see things differently. Samson whose name means sunshine and whose life was programmed to bring rays of sunshine to his parents after a long season of barrenness, as well as to shine the sun of victory over Israel after a long season of defeat and oppression, failed miserably because he lacked proper focus. He became so self focused that he never saw the big picture of what his life could have accomplished for God. Manoah his father and Samson's mum must have brought him up in the strict observance of the instructions given to them by God, his diet, appearance and companions were restricted and perhaps being an only child, with long hair like a girl may have led to him being a spoilt child. But it was soon evident that Samson had a huge problem with self-identity. He got an understanding of his call from his parents but never sought God himself to develop and clarify his purpose. He never sought to define his identity and obtain God's strategies and directions for his life. This was the greatest failure of this great leader of Israel.

A warrior understands that focus is what enables you to receive the spiritual vision that God has earmarked for you and that receiving the vision ultimately changes the lens with which you see the world. In Samson's case, because he did not seek to receive what to focus on from God, he focused on himself. The very first thing we hear about him in his adult life was that he wanted a girl. If his focus was different and he had concentrated on what God wanted him to do, he would have acquired the wisdom of big-picture thinking, learned the power of focused thinking and become more creative and strategic in his approach to life. For instance, if we compare Samson's approach to his assignment with Nehemiah's approach, we discover that the big difference was that while one sought God for how to go about the assignment, the other kind of stumbled through it.

Samson's life teaches us that without proper focus we can

make up an agenda and set goals by the sheer power of our human will, intelligence and ingenuity that is contrary to God's will. We can make things happen but those things will happen on a different scale than if our focus has its root embedded in the full understanding of our identity. When you understand a God vision and are assured of God's backing and leading you will make maximum impact. Life is more than just chance and those who choose to live by chance will be subject to many things not within their control. Life is ruled by the choices we make. Samson had a destiny that was clearcut for him before he was born but he did not allow God to lead him; he was led by wrong choices, wrong passions and sheer lust. He refused to focus. Although Samson did not develop a clear identity around God's purpose and vision for his life, he was all God had and because God is not wasteful or stupid God still worked with Samson's weakness and lack of focus to achieve His purpose. I believe that if Samson had developed an identity and clarity about his purpose and understood the reasons for his gifts he would have made different choices and lived a different lifestyle. He would have become a different kind of leader. If Samson had sought God and accepted responsibility for his gifts, it would have refined his tastes and character and God would have used him in a different way. Instead of being a one-man riot squad whose fights centered on women, he could have galvanized the whole nation, trained and raised an army and won more long time strategic victory for Israel. The Holy Spirit could have led him into making wiser decisions but his pleasure loving, sex driven passions led him another way.

The horrible fact is that it was not until Samson eyes were gouged out and he became blind physically that he received spiritual vision, it was not until he could no longer be distracted by the carnal nature that he was able to look within and discern his spiritual purpose. What he saw of God within made him more aware of himself as he related to God, he found and understood the depth of God's mercy and forgiveness and he humbled himself. Instead of picking fights based on his sense of outrage or desire for revenge because he was wronged, he came into the understanding of God's higher purpose for his gift.

Lessons on Focus

If you want a God-dream, or want to receive a picture of your future from God, work on your character and pray for a loving heart. You will always see things differently from a pure heart than a biased one. If you want God to reveal your future spend time with Him, it's not enough to read the bible and books written by others, it is also important to spend time in God's presence in worship. I believe God is more interested in deepening His relationship with you than seeing you achieve whatever you are trying to accomplish. You are His workmanship; God has prepared you for good works so begin to patiently seek God's revelation for your life so that you are aimed at something. True success is becoming who God wants you to be. It is accomplishing the goals God helps you to set. This requires focus. Focus will help you appreciate your gifts and talents. It will also enable you to identify and starve your weaknesses by taking them to God and asking for His help.

Discipline

The warrior embraces personal discipline in order to discover what God has put in him or her to make them of maximum benefit to mankind and to God's creation. The heroes of faith in Hebrews 11 had the warriors mindset; these were men and women who believed the truth of God and faced circumstances and challenges with courageous strength - Abraham, Isaac, Jacob, Joseph, Moses, Joshua, Rahab, Gideon, Barak, Deborah, Samson, Jephthah, David, Samuel, Daniel and others. The hallmark of their lives and indeed what should be that of every Christian life, as a soldier of Christ must be self-discipline. God hates indiscipline.

"You therefore must endure hardship as a good soldier of Jesus Christ. No one engaged in warfare entangles himself with the affairs of this life, that he may please him who enlisted him as a soldier." 2 Timothy 2:3-4 NKJV

> *"But I discipline my body and bring it into subjection, lest, when I have preached to others, I myself should become disqualified."*
> *1 Corinthians 9:27*

Assertiveness

A warrior is always practical and assertive; he or she understands the necessity of 'provoking' a war with the enemy when it is due. Warriors have a hatred for procrastination. They are motivated by God's promises to move forward in a resolute way. A warrior develops the ability to weigh situations, analyse resources and evaluate how to combine skills and resources to overcome his opponent in order to gain the victory. The warrior sets out to understand the weapons of his opponent and then strategically maps out a way to have the edge and win the fight. Therefore a warrior's life is active, you are not to sit and wait for things to happen, you do your best to make things happen. This is the difference between the warrior and the ordinary soldier. While a soldier obeys the commands of his superiors, he is often not required to do strategic thinking. Strategic thinking is the privilege of the officers; they plan the supply lines, the right positions and timing of attacks and retreat. The senior officer is qualified to command because of developed skills not only in the art of combat but also critical and strategic thinking. God wants you to pray and learn how to think. Prayer, fasting and thinking through with God is what gets us the victory.

> *"Come now, and let us reason together,"*
> *Says the LORD,*
> *"Though your sins are like scarlet,*
> *They shall be as white as snow;*
> *Though they are red like crimson,*
> *They shall be as wool."*
> *Isaiah 1:18 NKJV*

Persistence

To succeed as a warrior is to understand the virtue of persistence; this is because too many people give up too soon. Warriors develop patience and persistence as an attitude and way of life. They are ready and prepared to face difficulties, pain, discomfort, discouragement, fear and the prospect of failure without giving up. They recognize that men and women of wonder and distinction are not born, they are made; they are those who learn to exercise themselves in the conditions and attitudes that guarantee and establish wonder. This is precisely what qualifies them as warriors.

Persistence is tenacity of purpose, an attitude of refusing

to be discouraged. Sometimes to win the race, you don't need great education although it is important to have one, you often don't need great charm and connection either or even deep spiritual understanding, all you need is a persistent determination.

Those who are easily moved, who give up easily never attain much. Many have abandoned a course because they faced a seemingly insurmountable challenge but the warrior knows that the presence of a challenge does not imply you are not in God's will. Those who breakthrough never let go because of the comment or opinion of others. Giving up is picking up the ticket to failure. The warrior is determined not to faint or be weary because their focus is on the harvest or end result.

> *"But Jesus said to him, "No one, having put his hand to the plow, and looking back, is fit for the kingdom of God."*
> *Luke 9:62 NKJV*

Not fit for the kingdom if you look back? Yes, that is because the God of the kingdom doesn't look back. He never gives up on you. God will never give up on you as long as you don't turn your back on Him. If you know and understand the value of redemption and you know the greatness of the God who is behind you and cheering you on, you will never give up. Why give up? Listen to Paul, he said he was beaten, ship wrecked and suffered untold hardships but nothing could separate him from the love of God. What can ever make you give up when you know victory is assured? Well, if you are born again and the Spirit of God is in you, nothing is strong enough to break your spirit or make you give up.

Faith by definition is an attitude, a commitment to the integrity of God's words. It is commitment that provokes the omnipotence of God. Patience and persistence is what demonstrates your unshakeable confidence in the immutability of God's counsel. It also demonstrates an understanding of the depth of God's love for you.

> *"That you do not become sluggish, but imitate those who through faith and patience inherit the promises. ... And so, after he had patiently endured, he obtained the promise."*
> Hebrews 6:12,15 NKJV

> *"For you have need of endurance, so that after you have done the will of God, you may receive the promise:"*
> Hebrews 10:36 NKJV

> *"But without faith it is impossible to please Him, for he who comes to God must believe that He is, and that He is a rewarder of those who diligently seek Him."*
> Hebrews 11:6 NKJV

The warrior knows that all warfare and conflict is first won in the mind before any physical resolution is made because victory or defeat is more a matter of spiritual disposition than physical prowess. The warrior is keenly aware that no one is defeated as long as their spirit is unbroken. When a warrior fails at a task without giving up or surrendering, his spirit actually becomes stronger to fight harder the next time.

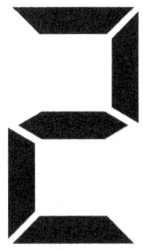

WARRIORS CONTEND

To enjoy a life of breakthrough, you must know how to contend in the right way for your spiritual inheritance. You are blessed already with all spiritual blessings in heavenly places in Christ. [Ephesians 1:3] But it takes insight, understanding and determination to know and appropriate the requisite behavior that demonstrates to your opposition that you are aware of and believe your victory in God. Great faith is not only a result of great revelation but of great dedication to the revelation of truth. It is your rugged determination to contend with the truth you believe in that produces results.

In the Pauline epistles, the subject of the apostle's passionate prayer was for those who believe to receive wisdom and understanding in the knowledge of God so they can be empowered to walk in all their inheritance in God. It is important on a personal basis to understand how to stand as a warrior who overcomes, because the opposition and whatever causes the difficulties in your life will not assume that you know you are an over comer. When you don't know what belongs to you, it holds no value to you; it is almost the same as it not belonging to you. But if you understand what belongs to you and yet sit down passively, it is even worse; it becomes an abuse of that knowledge. There is no one who ever amounted to anything in life who did not contend for something.

> *"Set out now and cross the Arnon Gorge. See, I have given into your hand Sihon the Amorite, king of Heshbon, and his country. Begin to take possession of it and engage him in battle."*
> *Deuteronomy 2:24 NIV*

> *"Get ready and set out for the Wadi Arnon. Look! I've given into your control Sihon the Amorite, king of Heshbon, along with his land. Prepare to take possession by provoking him to war."*
> *Deuteronomy 2:24 ISV*

God's instruction is quite clear here, He says, He has 'given' this territory to the Israelites but they were to take possession of this inheritance by engaging with the opposition in battle; the International Standard Version says by 'provoking' to war. Though God gave a guarantee that the land should be their own, yet they must contend with the enemy and provoke the opposition so they can get at what God has promised. Whatever God gives, you must venture out to get or receive. The implications are many here and one of them is that, certain things may belong to you, but they never become yours until you are willing to fight for them. You must think like a warrior and be ready to provoke a fight if required.

> *"This day I will begin to put the dread and fear of you upon the*

nations under the whole heaven, who shall hear the report of you, and shall tremble and be in anguish because of you."
Deuteronomy 2:25 NKJV

You are not the one to fear, God has put fear and dread in the heart of your enemy so do not fear. There are times when the roar of the Lion of the tribe of Judah is within you but you run helter-skelter from a fake lion that has no teeth. No! God wants you to stand your ground and roar back, "Enough." Until you resist the enemy you never know how much power you can exercise and how weak he is. Resist him and he will flee from you. He who put the dread and fear inside the devil is called Jesus Christ and you are His perfect image. The Christ who routed Satan, who made an open show of him, who took back power and authority from him now lives in you. There is a fear and dread of you in the realm of darkness because light dwells within you and that light shines in darkness and darkness cannot comprehend it. Your light has its source in God and therefore darkness cannot handle you. Wow! It is time exercise the light and amazing power inside you.

You are called by God to live for His purpose and you must rise up to that position of destiny in Jesus name. You are called to stand strong in the midst of a fallen world. Even as warfare rages and Satan works day and night to prevent you from advancing the kingdom of God, always remember that you are called to demonstrate Christ's victory over the deception and wiles of the devil.

"But even if our gospel is veiled, it is veiled to those who are perishing, whose minds the god of this age has blinded, who do not believe, lest the light of the gospel of the glory of Christ, who is the image of God, should shine on them."
2 Corinthians 4:3-4 NKJV

The battle we fight with Satan is for the souls of men; Satan's objective is to blindfold those who are perishing until they perish beyond redemption. In the same way, he tries to stop those who believe from advancing the victory of the kingdom of God. But you can destroy the tactics and devices of the enemy because you have received the power to overcome every attack and obstacle and to move forward with clarity and confidence. You must develop confidence that is based on the word of God. As you submit to His word, you gain the strength you need to move forward with authority and to triumph. Your enemy wants to keep you and those around you blind and discouraged. However God has chosen you to be a co-labourer with Him, to rescue the perishing and bring light to dark situations. Be aware that it is only in the process of warfare that you will mature. It is opposition that makes you stronger; the Holy Spirit in our struggles helps us to conform to the image of Christ as He intercedes for us and helps us to pray.

This battle is fought on two planes, in the unseen heavenly dimension, and in the equally unseen battlefield of the mind. Whatever we see in the physical world is a by-product of events taking place in the unseen spirit realm. Whenever people come to salvation on earth, their minds begin to see life from an eternal perspective, a different dimension that receives wisdom and discretion not only from the present but also from the future. As more people turn to the light, territory is taken away from Satan and his cohorts.

> *"For though we walk in the flesh, we do not war according to the flesh. For the weapons of our warfare are not carnal but mighty in God for pulling down strongholds, casting down arguments and every high thing that exalts itself against the knowledge of God, bringing every thought into captivity to the obedience of Christ,*

and being ready to punish all disobedience when your obedience is fulfilled."
2 Corinthians 10:3-6 NKJV

"For we do not wrestle against flesh and blood, but against principalities, against powers, against the rulers of the darkness of this age, against spiritual hosts of wickedness in the heavenly places.
Ephesians 6:12 NKJV

"And I will give you the keys of the kingdom of heaven, and whatever you bind on earth will be bound in heaven, and whatever you loose on earth will be loosed in heaven."
Matthew 16:19 NKJV

Always remember that if you are a believer in Christ, you are fighting from a position of victory, you are not just fighting to win, you are fighting to defend a victory that is won already and handed to you by Jesus Christ. Satan knows your position and his main strategy is to deceive you and convince you to fight for victory rather than to advance forward in the victory of Christ. You have been given authority and it is time for you to exercise it.

"Then the seventy returned with joy, saying, "Lord, even the demons are subject to us in Your name. And He said to them, "I saw Satan fall like lightning from heaven. "Behold, I give you the authority to trample on serpents and scorpions, and over all the power of the enemy, and nothing shall by any means hurt you."
Luke 10:17-19 NKJV

"In Him you also trusted, after you heard the word of truth, the gospel of your salvation; in whom also, having believed, you were sealed with the Holy Spirit of promise, who is the guarantee of our inheritance until the redemption of the purchased possession, to the

praise of His glory."
Ephesians 1:13-14 NKJV

Let's take another look the scriptures we started with: 1 John 5:4 seems to be connected to several other scriptures that establish the victory of those who belong to the kingdom of God.

"But as many as received Him, to them He gave the right to become children of God, to those who believe in His name: who were born, not of blood, nor of the will of the flesh, nor of the will of man, but of God."
John 1:12-13 NKJV

"Jesus answered and said to him, "Most assuredly, I say to you, unless one is born again, he cannot see the kingdom of God."
John 3:3 NKJV

"But thanks be to God, who gives us the victory through our Lord Jesus Christ."
1 Corinthians 15:57 NKJV

"You are of God, little children, and have overcome them, because He who is in you is greater than he who is in the world."
1 John 4:4 NKJV

What does this imply? The world or cosmos stands for a system that is opposed to keeping the commandments of God and draws us away from God. There are certain precepts and customs typical of this world system that should not rule the life of a child of God. To be born of God implies that we share in the victory of Christ by faith. What did Christ overcome? He overcame Satan, the god of this world, the lusts in the world, false prophets and wicked men who by temptations and threatening and evil doctrines try to stop you from obeying God. This is the victory we are offered in Christ.

There is total victory of our faith when it is in Christ Jesus. Christ brings us salvation because of the grace freely given to us by God, but even more we have access to His life and power when Christ becomes the object of our faith. The moment we were brought into union with Christ our victory was won and secured. We become as He is (1 John 4:17); we become partakers of His victory (John 16:33); we become partakers of His glory (John 17:22) and He becomes the greater one in us (1 John 4:4)

It is as your faith grows in strength that the world loses its power over you. Faith is a spiritual sensory organ that enables you to engage with another realm, a realm that is supernatural but is as real and true as that which your physical sense reveals. Just as a child begins to feed off and believe information from the senses, so the Bible tells us about feeding on the word,

"So then faith comes by hearing, and hearing by the word of God."
Romans 10:17 NKJV

Authority to Contend

There is the story of a Roman centurion who met Jesus. [Matthew 8:5-13; Luke 7:1-10] This was not a parable but a true story and Jesus who is the Truth, commended this man for having great faith. This commendation was because the man had an understanding of authority. He was a soldier in charge of 100 men who would not dare disobey his orders. How does being a soldier and the understanding of authority help your faith? First, it is important for you to understand that you are called to be a soldier and to be a good soldier you must understand what it means to be a soldier. A soldier obeys orders. It is important to understand the delegation of authority, because you will gain more confidence in your contending with the enemy. A warrior fully understands the source of his or her authority.

> *"You therefore must endure hardship as a good soldier of Jesus Christ. No one engaged in warfare entangles himself with the affairs of this life, that he may please him who enlisted him as a soldier."*
> *2 Timothy 2:3-4 NKJV*

There are three things Paul states in this verse, first, we are soldiers of Christ and warriors of righteousness; second, Christ chooses us and our duty is to please Christ who chose us.

What is Authority?

Authority is delegated influence, an ability given, a privilege bestowed, a force or capacity or competence to take control on behalf of another. It is entrusted or permissible power. There are two words in Greek that expresses this thought. Exousia or authority is a noun and Katexousiazo the exercise of authority is a verb. While authority is a great concept, it has no benefit except it is exercised, which is why we need an understanding of how to exercise our authority in Christ.

> *"For whatever is born of God overcomes the world. And this is the victory that has overcome the world our faith. Who is he who overcomes the world, but he who believes that Jesus is the Son of God?"*
> *1 John 5:4-5 NKJV*

Our faith in Jesus is demonstrated in our submission to His authority, what we believe is what we strive to become. When we are born of God we have the potential to overcome, we receive Exousia but we need to exercise it by faith, it must become Katexousiazo for us to overcome. In the book of Revelations we are commanded to overcome because from Genesis to Revelation God has not changed in His original intention for man to have dominion and to walk in victory over every situation. Listen to the very first words man ever heard from God

> *"Then God blessed them, and God said to them, "Be fruitful and multiply; fill the earth and subdue it; have dominion over the fish of the sea, over the birds of the air, and over every living thing that moves on the earth."*
> *Genesis 1:28 NKJV*

This is delegated authority, the word subdue means to tread down, to conquer, to subjugate, to keep under. In trying to understand this word I found some other places where it was used apart from the creation narration.

In 1 Chronicles 17:10, a variation of the word subdue expresses the thought of vanquishing an enemy and to bring down opposition. In Psalm 47:3, it is used to connote victory through an arrangement of words, by speaking, to subdue by an answer, a command or declaration. In Isaiah 45:1, it meant to tread to pieces, to rule and have dominion over.

This led me to conclude that the mouth and feet are crucial to the exercise of authority and contending with the enemy of our soul. When we encounter the word 'subdue' in the New Testament in its Greek expression in 1 Corinthians15: 20-28, it is used in simple demonstration of how God has brought all things under Christ through His word.

> "And He put all things under His feet, and gave Him to be head over all things to the church,"
> Ephesians 1:22 NKJV

> "You have put all things in subjection under his feet." For in that He put all in subjection under him, He left nothing that is not put under him. But now we do not yet see all things put under him."
> Hebrews 2:8 NKJV

In the Greek, the word subdue is Huppotasso, a compound word that means to put under and arrange. Huppo means to put under and Tasso means to arrange.
Therefore to subdue connotes the putting under or the subordination of something by some form of arrangement. If we consider that God has brought all things under Christ who is the full expression of His word as established by John 1:1-14; Psalm 138:2 and Philippians 3:20-21 we can conclude that the instrument of contention, of dominion or subjugation is the mouth and all authority is exercised by words.

The feet are used in the same manner; your feet are the instrument of possession because your words are empowered by the dignity of your walk. Words are only as powerful as the integrity of the one who speaks them. Our walk is figurative of our character and inner development. Therefore, to win in the battles of life you must arrange with your mouth what you intend to possess with your feet and always remember that your words are only as powerful as your walk.

> "Indeed My hand has laid the foundation of the earth,
> And My right hand has stretched out the heavens;
> When I call to them,

They stand up together."
Isaiah 48:13 NKJV

There is a walk and a work that precedes the calling out in faith for manifestation. God has brought all things under Christ (His Word) and Christ has all things under control through the words He has spoken to us. The first man Adam in Genesis 2:7 was made a living soul, he derived life from God but Jesus Christ the last Adam came as a life giving spirit. He is a fountain of life giving life to others. Jesus said in effect that His words give life and spirit to the recreated man and woman. [John 1:4; John 5:21; John 6:63; John 10:10; John 12:24]

"As His divine power has given to us all things that pertain to life and godliness, through the knowledge of Him who called us by glory and virtue, by which have been given to us exceedingly great and precious promises, that through these you may be partakers of the divine nature, having escaped the corruption that is in the world through lust."
2 Peter 1:3-4 NKJV

The first man is of the earth, the second from heaven, each is head of a creation but as in Adam all die, in Christ all shall be made alive. The promises of God provide us incorruptible weapons for our contention and victory.

Confession

I refuse to be a victim of life and by the Blood of Jesus I declare that I am delivered out of every trap and every grave. Every appointment with death is destroyed because Christ came to give me abundant life, I will live to fulfill my days. The Lord Himself shall defend me and I shall be far from oppression within and without. The Lord will confirm the Blood covering over my life with signs and wonders. I declare my freedom and liberty to serve God in good health and with abundant wealth for the rest of my life. I receive baptism into good old age in Jesus name. Satan I come against you by the Blood of Jesus and I declare you have no part with me, no part with my family and career, my business and my spiritual life. I declare everything that is against me must bow to the resurrection power of the Blood of Jesus today. God is for me, He has justified me by the Blood, no one can be against me, what is past is past the devil cannot condemn me. I receive inexplicable favour. I receive power that will make my enemies bow, riches to separate me from poverty and shame, wisdom to make me shine in the midst of darkness, strength to do exploits when men are distressed, honour to distinguish me when others are put to shame, glory to make me a wonder and the blessings of God that add no sorrows.

WARRIORS RENEW THEIR MIND

> *"I beseech you therefore, brethren, by the mercies of God, that you present your bodies a living sacrifice, holy, acceptable to God, which is your reasonable service. And do not be conformed to this world, but be transformed by the renewing of your mind, that you may prove what is that good and acceptable and perfect will of God."*
> Romans 12:1-2 NKJV

The word "conform" means to put on the form, fashion, or appearance of another. It may refer to anything pertaining to the habit, manner, dress, style of living, etc., of others. The 'world' as used in this scripture does not just refer to the physical world but an age or generation and its maxims, thoughts, feelings, prevailing habits, style and manners.

Your soul is your mind, emotions and will; it is the seat of your decision-making. When you make right decisions it leads to a right destiny, this is why God stresses transformation through the renewing of the mind. To have a renewed mind is being totally submitted to the Holy Spirit in your spirit. A renewed mind enables you to act from your communication with God instead of your physical senses and carnal thinking.

Whatever controls your soul will determine the course of your life because God will respect your free will. However, Satan has not changed his tactics; he wants you to take on what is God's responsibility and to devise your own way, which ultimately leads to pride. The Christian church is always in danger of being infiltrated by the spirit of secularism. Don't let the world around you squeeze you into its own mould but rather let God be the one to shape your mind and perspectives.

The Christian warrior fights the deception of the enemy because that is the greatest threat to victory. The Bible warns that even the very elect can be deceived. But there is a solution to deception, it is found in having a passionate commitment to the truth of the word of God. [2 Thessalonians 2:10-12; Ephesians 2: 2-6; Romans 5:17] We are already positional joint heirs with Christ; seated with Him in heavenly places far above all the power of the enemy. This is a position of authority, honour and triumph not of failure and defeat.

But why are we still subject to Satan and his deceptions?

"To them God willed to make known what are the riches of the glory of this mystery among the Gentiles: which is Christ in you, the hope of glory. Him we preach, warning every man and teaching every man in all wisdom, that we may present every man perfect in Christ Jesus. To this end I also labor, striving according to His working

which works in me mightily."
Colossians 1:27-29 NKJV

There are three aspects to the renewing of your mind and your perfection in Christ. You must accept that Christ came and obtained a new nature for all members of His body, this nature is His own life, which He perfected through suffering and obedience. You must believe that you can be perfected in Christ because of the Holy Spirit who unites you with Christ, this is a life planted in you as a seed the moment you receive Jesus Christ as Lord and Saviour. This is 'Zoe' life in itself, it is planted as seed into our sinful flesh with the power to grow and fill our life with fruit of righteousness unto perfection. The third step is the due process of patience that enables the growing into perfection through the first two steps described. When you obey in faith and appropriate what you have received and yield yourself to the truth revealed so that revealed truth becomes your life and conduct, then the word of God that you receive, read, study, and meditate on begins to work powerfully in your life to establish and perfect God's purpose. [1 Thessalonians 5:23; Hebrews 4:12]

The nature of the flesh gives the devil access through the physical senses into our soul, our thoughts, reason and emotions. The only way to exercise victory over the devil is to allow your spirit man to have dominion. As long as you are in the body, you will have the desires of the flesh and the unredeemed soul to fight and this is the realm where Satan will try to defeat you. Evil spirits are real and they seek to oppress, obsess and if possible posses mankind. You are a spirit being with a soul who lives through a body. The true warrior wages a war of discipline on the flesh by staying close to the Holy Spirit in prayer and meditating in the word.

The greatest way to keep yourself out of trouble and to stay victorious is to watch what comes out of your mouth. I often say that the Apostle Paul through the incredible wisdom and revelation given to him by God laid out for us the syllabus of the New Testament life in his letter to the Philippians,

> *"Finally, brethren, whatever things are true, whatever things are noble, whatever things are just, whatever things are pure, whatever things are lovely, whatever things are of good report, if there is any virtue and if there is anything praiseworthy—meditate on these things."*
> Philippians 4:8 NKJV

The devil knows that whatever you fix your mind on and think of, you will eventually speak out. Satan knows he can only do what we permit him to do, so if you speak evil or trouble, you give him permission. If a wrong thought comes into your mind, the Bible says lay your hand upon your mouth, don't speak it out. The devil will plant a thought and urge you to release it into the earth by saying it. If you can take control of your mind by subjecting that thought to God's holy word and speaking God's word instead you will enjoy continuous victory. [Proverbs 21:23; 30:32; Psalm 50:1; James 1:21-22; 4:7]

James tells us that the only thing that can save our soul or develop our mind to a state where it can function at the same kind of frequency with the Holy Spirit, who dwells within us, is to become familiar with the word of God. We engraft the word or implant what can change our minds and emotions through reading it, meditating or thinking about it and then speaking out the promises of God in His word. To save is defined as, to deliver, protect, heal, preserve, make well and make whole - your soul is your greatest asset and defense against Satan because when your soul is sound, your words will be wholesome.

> *"Since you have purified your souls in obeying the truth through the Spirit in sincere love of the brethren, love one another fervently with a pure heart,"*
> 1 Peter 1:22 NKJV

Until you do what the word says, it cannot profit you. The truth begins to profit you when you declare it and do it; we practice it by speaking it and that leads us to behave it. We must understand that the word of God is food for the spirit, the purer your heart the purer you will see; the purer your conscience, the greater your boldness and the exercise of your faith. There is the life of God contained in His word that empowers and delivers the abilities of God into every situation when it is introduced into that situation. [Luke 4:4; John 6:63; Jude 1:20] God gives us clear instructions on how to keep our minds and spirits strong. We must keep our minds and thoughts focused on God. The reason God tells us to change our thinking is that man's mind is the first place where Satan tries to gain access, even the minds of Christians who let him. [Isaiah26: 3; Philippians 4:6-8]

Satan's method is to make you feel discouraged, worthless and hopeless in whatever challenge you face. Discouragement and depression does not happen overnight but gradually, it builds up a thought at a time and before you know it you are sad and lacking energy. But the secret war of the warrior is the war of worship and prayer; the warrior through prayer receives the power of sanctification and stays ahead by asking God in preparation today for the wonders of tomorrow. The easiest way the enemy makes people loose balance is through anger and strife, which results from pride.

"Where do wars and fights come from among you? Do they not come from your desires for pleasure that war in your members?"
James 4:1 NKJV

This scripture written by James makes a very bold assertion that strife and all forms of contention have one source - lust. The letter was written to Christians as a warning to safeguard them from a spirit prevailing among the Jews at that time. Historians tell us this was a time when the Jews under the pretense of defending their religion and fighting for the liberty they believed they were entitled to, rebelled against the Roman rule. This led to a lot of bloodshed and misery but because they were also divided into many factions, they split into several groups amongst themselves and they had such violent contentions that they plundered and massacred each other. Their actions were based on covetousness; they had a pretended zeal, which was a shelter for pride, malice, ambition and even revenge. The secret war of the warrior includes meditative prayer that keeps the mind humble and dependent on God.

On the other hand, there is lust, which is defined as an overwhelming desire or craving usually for sex or power, an eagerness or enthusiasm bothering on obsession. On a larger scale it is the source of wars, struggle for wealth, resources, territory, ambition, fame or more extended dominion and it is what prompted the conquest of Alexander the Great, Julius Caesar, Napoleon Bonaparte and Adolf Hitler. These men had a pretended zeal that sheltered covetousness, pride, malice, ambition, revenge and so on. On a smaller scale, lust also wars in our members. The word members refer to our body, our flesh, because it is the seat of our desires and passions. The warrior understands that only by submitting to and conquering the war within through prayer can we win the war without.

There is a war going on between our passions and desires and our conscience or spirit. Love of conquest, gratification of senses, revenge and ambition for extended rule and other such issues have led to war on a global scale, but these same things cause war in our hearts. [Romans 6:13; Romans 6:19; Romans 7:5; Romans 7:23]

These lusts in the flesh sometimes exercise such force or power that all our sense of justice, equity, even the fear of God are often thrown aside in its pursuit. The lie or presupposition of war is that a wrong has been done on one side or the other or on both sides. Perceived wrong or offence is dangerous. The warrior understands the power of grace and plans to forgive others ahead of any offence committed. The warrior does not engage in warfare because of a perceived offence. The warrior understands that the opposition is often spiritual and not physical. [Hebrews 12:5] The first sign of natural corruption is envy, this is defined as a resentful emotion that occurs when a person lacks another's perceived superior quality achievement or possession and either desires it or wishes the other lacked it.

When lust has its grip on a mind, it will not allow contentment or satisfaction. The crowd of sinful desires and affections will stop prayerfulness and the working of our desires toward God. The warrior knows this and will do everything to win the secret battle of prayer that keeps the mind stayed on God and His word. Lust is a manifestation of pride because it resists God in our understanding. Lust will resist the truth of God and the laws of God and the providence of God and make you think God is against you.

Confession:

I come against spiritual coldness, luke-warmness and prayerlessness in my life and I pull down strongholds, imaginations and everything projected by satanic hosts against my spirit, soul and body in Jesus name. I reject every plan to make me a prey of the terrible and captive of the mighty in Jesus name and I return every dart and arrow, enchantment, divination, spells and sorcery against my life in Jesus name. I refuse to be entangled by the snare of bitterness, un-forgiveness, envy, jealousy, strife, anger, fear and doubt and whatever would hinder my prayers and communion with God. The Lord God is my head cover in the days of battle. I release everyone who has offended me in Jesus name and I bind every strange acquaintance and any enemy pretending as friend whose mouth speak vanity and whose right hand is a right-hand of falsehood. I am the righteousness of God in Christ and neutralize the spirits of envy, jealousy, lust, lies and hatred in my life in Jesus name. I am redeemed by the blood of Jesus and kept by the power of God.

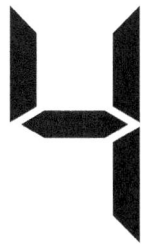

HOW TO EXERCISE YOUR SPIRIT AND PREVAIL

"So mightily grew the word of God and prevailed"
Acts 19:20 NKJV

The result of renewing the mind is a soul that is exercised by the spirit and so becomes empowered for victory. In the passage above, a statement is made of the power and efficacy of the word of God. When Paul arrived at Ephesus in Acts 19 it was to fulfill the promise he had made to them in Acts 18:21. Ephesus at this time was one of the largest cities in the Mediterranean world. It was famous for the temple of Artemis and the worship of Diana. Ephesus in the Roman world was a centre for black magic and occult practices, which were all organised for profit. This was a society that looked to sorcery and magic to get wealth, to be happy and become successful. It was into this historical context that Paul arrived and after baptising some disciples so that they received the Holy Spirit he began to teach the word of Christ and God began to confirm the word he taught with signs and wonders.

Into this scenario arrived also the sons of Sceva, their father was a notable chief among the priests and when they attempted to use the name of Jesus like a magic incantation without being a disciple of the word, they were thoroughly whipped by the devil. This resulted in many people burning their magic books and other occult paraphernalia. Therefore the word of God grew and prevailed over conjuring books, conjurers, the devil and all powers of darkness.

The primary message was that the Word of God would prevail in and through those who are disciples of the Word.

There are two words that stand out in this text: the words "grew" and "prevail" - grew is the simple past tense of grow, which means to increase by natural development, by assimilation and nourishment. It also means to bring forth, to advance and increase. Prevail on the one hand means to become widespread and on the other hand it means to predominate, to be superior in strength, in power and influence, to succeed and have dominion, to rule, reign and restrain. To exercise power or force, exhibit strength and ability, to have efficacy and value, to conquer.

These two words define or describe the nature of God's word. The word of God - what God speaks, what God has said, whether it is a promise, commandment, instruction, warning, law or gospel has living power that produces result. The revelations of God and the will of God are active, living and able to penetrate and prevail over all things.

> *"For the word of God is quick, and powerful, and sharper than any two-edged sword, piercing even to the dividing asunder of soul and spirit, and of the joints and marrow, and is a discerner of the thoughts and intents of the heart."*
> *Hebrews 4:12*

The word of God is alive, it brings life to us, it has the power to penetrate deep into your bone marrow and rearrange your cell structure or affect your blood flow. It also has the power to change how you think. Satan's greatest strategy is to stop you from hearing what God is saying to you. God's word is primarily creative and is always accompanied with power but Satan only steals, kills and destroys.

> *"In the beginning was the Word, and the Word was with God, and the Word was God. The same was in the beginning with God. All things were made by him; and without him was not any thing made that was made. In him was life; and the life was the light of men. And the light shineth in darkness; and the darkness comprehended it not."*
> *John 1:1-5 NKJV*

Everything created was created by the word of God and everything in the kingdom of God is operated by the word of God. We live in a word created universe and a word-governed system. You cannot separate God from His words and you will live or die under the authority of the words you speak or the words you hear and believe. Your life is primarily governed by words.

> *"It is the Spirit who gives life; the flesh profits nothing. The words that I speak to you are spirit, and they are life."*
> *John 6:63 NKJV*

It is interesting to observe the comparison between the following scriptures:

> *"And this continued for two years, so that all who dwelt in Asia heard the word of the Lord Jesus, both Jews and Greeks. Now God worked unusual miracles by the hands of Paul, so that even handkerchiefs or aprons were brought from his body to the sick, and the diseases left them and the evil spirits went out of them."*
> Acts 19:10-12 NKJV

> *"And they went out and preached everywhere, the Lord working with them and confirming the word through the accompanying signs. Amen"*
> Mark 16:20 NKJV

> *"Now it happened on a certain day, as He was teaching, that there were Pharisees and teachers of the law sitting by, who had come out of every town of Galilee, Judea, and Jerusalem. And the power of the Lord was present to heal them."*
> Luke 5:17 NKJV

> "For I am not ashamed of the gospel of Christ,fn for it is the power of God to salvation for everyone who believes, for the Jew first and also for the Greek." Romans 1:16

> "But to those who are called, both Jews and Greeks, Christ the power of God and the wisdom of God."
> 1 Corinthians 1:24 NKJV

Miracles confirm the word, God said I will not break my covenant nor alter the words from my mouth, and since God cannot deny Himself, He manifests His power wherever His word is proclaimed. He delights to confirm His words. Where

His word is present there is power to heal and deliver. His word is made to us His wisdom and power. Every key of the kingdom is operated by the word of God. To operate in the supernatural realm for instance Jesus gave us an insight from John 3:8

" *"The wind blows where it wishes, and you hear the sound of it, but cannot tell where it comes from and where it goes. So is everyone who is born of the Spirit."*
John 3:8 NKJV

Signs follow the sounds we make, as long as we make sounds reflecting God's words we become unstoppable by negative spiritual forces.

In the realm of our health, Proverbs 4:22 declares concerning God's word,
"For they are life to those who find them, And health to all their flesh." NKJV

Even the arena of prayer is also governed by His word, 1 John 5:14 says,

"Now this is the confidence that we have in Him, that if we ask anything according to His will, He hears us."
NKJV

Our desire for success is determined according to Joshua 1:8 by God's word,

"This Book of the Law shall not depart from your mouth, but you shall meditate in it day and night, that you may observe to do according to all that is written in it. For then you will make your way prosperous, and then you will have good success."
NKJV

That which pleases God the most is built up in us by His word – Faith; Romans 10:17 declares,

> *"So then faith comes by hearing, and hearing by the word of God."*
> *NKJV*

Fulfilling our destiny of Holiness/Sanctification and becoming like Christ is a function also of giving God's word its place of primacy in our lives John 17:17, "Sanctify them by Your truth. Your word is truth." Psalm 119:9 say to us,

> *"How can a young man cleanse his way?*
> *By taking heed according to Your word."*
> *NKJV*

God's word remains the primary instrument of dominion, increase, replenishing and restoration on earth. It is only through the word that we can partake of and demonstrate God's divine nature.

> *"As His divine power has given to us all things that pertain to life and godliness, through the knowledge of Him who called us by glory and virtue, by which have been given to us exceedingly great and precious promises, that through these you may be partakers of the divine nature, having escaped the corruption that is in the world through lust."*
> *2 Peter 1:3-4 NKJV*

> *"So shall My word be that goes forth from My mouth; It shall not return to Me void, But it shall accomplish what I please, And it shall prosper in the thing for which I sent it. For you shall go out with joy, And be led out with peace; The mountains and the hills Shall break forth into singing before you, And all the trees of the field shall clap*

> their hands. *Instead of the thorn shall come up the cypress tree, And instead of the brier shall come up the myrtle tree; And it shall be to the LORD for a name, For an everlasting sign that shall not be cut off."*
> *Isaiah 55:11-13 NKJV*

This is a demonstration of the power of God's word to reverse the curse on the earth. When you lay hold on the word, you eliminate and avoid the curse so as to enter into the blessing and promises of God.

The main question to answer is how do you exercise your spirit with God's word so you can prevail in life? How do you allow the word to grow in you so you can have dominion? Our first insight is from 1 Timothy 4:8, Paul declares,

> *"For bodily exercise profits a little, but godliness is profitable for all things, having promise of the life that now is and of that which is to come."*
> *NKJV*

Paul hereby equates godliness to a form of exercise; exercise can be defined as any activity or training that develops the mind and body. It is often an activity that is planned, structured and repetitive for the purpose of conditioning any part of the body in order to improve health and fitness.

There are three basic types of fitness training: resistance training, endurance training and general toning exercises.

Resistance training

Hebrews 5:14 tell us,

"But solid food belongs to those who are of full age, that is, those who by reason of use have their senses exercised to discern both good and evil."
NKJV

So spiritual muscles can be exercised to grow, resistance training increases muscle strength by putting strain in the muscle. By definition, to resist is to stand against, to withstand, act in opposition, to counteract, to refuse to comply. Whenever you resist the devil you are actually growing your spiritual muscles. The apostles repeat this concept continuously.

"Therefore submit to God. Resist the devil and he will flee from you."
James 4:7 NKJV

"Be sober, be vigilant; because your adversary the devil walks about like a roaring lion, seeking whom he may devour. Resist him, steadfast in the faith, knowing that the same sufferings are experienced by your brotherhood in the world."
1 Peter 5:8-9 NKJV

Resistance starts with submission. To submit is to stand under the authority of another while to resist is to stand against. We gain the power of what we stand under to effectively resist what we stand against.

Jesus is our perfect example of resistance training. In the desert, he resisted presumption, pride, lust of the eyes and the promise of wealth. He submitted to the baptism of John the Baptist and stood under what was written in order to stand against the devil. Jesus came to reveal the Father to us and to establish a new covenant that says on this side of eternity you prevail by submitting to the word of God.

" By faith we understand that the worlds were framed by the word of God, so that the things which are seen were not made of things which are visible." Hebrews 11:3 NKJV

You can frame your world with the word of God as you submit to it and engage with it, you will develop appropriate spiritual muscles to deal with issues of life.

Endurance Training

To endure simply means to be able to stand strong in the face of opposition. Opposition is part of life. Your ability to prevail over opposition will depend on the quality of God's word that grows in your heart. Endurance is not about strength but stamina. Endurance is the power to withstand hardship, difficulties and opposition. The ability to refuse to quit knowing that if you don't give up you will eventually win.

"Therefore take up the whole armor of God, that you may be able to withstand in the evil day, and having done all, to stand."
Ephesians 6:13 NKJV

Paul says we should put on the whole armour of God and to stand, having done all we must stand in faith. To endure and build stamina you must do two things from Hebrews 12:1 3

"Therefore we also, since we are surrounded by so great a cloud of witnesses, let us lay aside every weight, and the sin which so easily ensnares us, and let us run with endurance the race that is set before

> *us, looking unto Jesus, the author and finisher of our faith, who for the joy that was set before Him endured the cross, despising the shame, and has sat down at the right hand of the throne of God. For consider Him who endured such hostility from sinners against Himself, lest you become weary and discouraged in your souls."*
> *Hebrews 12:1-3 NKJV*

You must put aside every unnecessary weight and sin that entangles. Extra weight will drain your strength, divert your focus and reduce the resources you have to reach your goal. You cannot be carrying someone else's load and finish your race at the right time. Neither can you be carrying something God says you should put down and finish at God's time.

How do you develop endurance? Endurance is built through an understanding of repentance. There are three stages to true repentance. The first stage is when you change your mind and turn away from sin. A change of mind opens a new season of transaction with heaven in your life. It opens up the fountains of mercy and forgiveness. Stage two is the fighting stage and it involves cutting off emotional ties from the past that can stop you from going into this new season. These soul ties are images and other sensory stimulus associated with past sin that is embedded in your mind and subconscious. Stage three begins when you have successfully cut those ties; and you have come to a place where you have put those memories under the blood such that they no longer resurface in your mind. There is no vacuum in nature therefore, repentance is not complete until you are able to take willful action in the opposite direction of what you turned from that produces the fruit of repentance. Cutting the soul ties with the source of sin and the grace to produce fruit in sync with the new season is what equates to spiritual endurance. The more you feed on the word and look unto Jesus the more established and secure you will become.

Toning Exercises

These are exercises that are not to build strength or stamina but to keep the entire body in working order. While in life there will be seasons where we go through God's boot camp to develop strength or stamina, toning exercises must be ongoing on a daily basis. These are the things we do consistently on a daily basis. Walking and swimming are said to be two of the best toning exercises.

The Bible has a lot to say about walking. Spiritually, walking refers to our manner of life, our character.

Galatians 5:15-16 says we should walk in the spirit.

Ephesians 5:15-16 walk circumspectly with wisdom redeeming the time.

Colossians 4:5 says walk with wisdom towards outsiders.

Finally, we must fellowship with the Holy Spirit and our Christian brethren. God said, it is not good that man should be alone; we are created and made for fellowship.

Philippians 2:2-8 demonstrates what happens in our lives when we fellowship with the Holy Spirit.
 - vs 2 - we become like minded with Christ
 - vs 3 - we become humble and teachable
 - vs 4 - we watch out and develop compassion for one another

- vs 7 - we develop a servants heart
- vs 8 - we become obedient to God

Through fellowship with the Holy Spirit we become more like Jesus Christ and all that He has becomes ours. It is your inheritance in Christ to be strong and victorious, never settle for anything less.

Confessions

From today I declare my faith in the promises of God. With my mouth I agree with God and release faith that will cause me to govern and have dominion over the field that God has given me. I declare that God is ordering my steps and my prayers are being guided by the Holy Spirit so that new paths of victory are forming before me. I will govern the treasures that God has given me. [Stretch out your hands before God] I declare that God will show me what He would have my hands to grasp, every resource around me that I have not yet seen, God will teach my hands to war and to prosper. God will teach me to lay my hand on the resources that will multiply and cause me to secure my future. [Walk around] I declare that my territory will be enlarged and I will posses all that God has in store for me.

Today I come into agreement with every word God is speaking into my future because I am ready for God to propel me forward with a new anointing and new favour/administration. Today I break soul ties with every weeping in the night and emotional trauma of the past. From today I declare I will rejoice. I declare, 'LET THERE BE LIGHT". Everything begins with light so I declare that God's divine light will penetrate the darkness in my future. Everything begins with light; my light has come for increase, breakthroughs, health and harvest! Let there be light. [Speak light into every aspect of your life]. Jesus came to destroy the works of darkness; therefore the light of Jesus will locate me and bring me into that place that God has called me to be. God will unravel my darkness, I shake off everything that has held back my destiny from its fullness, I shake off the darkness of the past season - shake it off now.

I will flow in the grace, the glory and the anointing of God. I am entering into my time of victory I declare that the spirit of victory is being released to me now in Jesus name. God will break loose upon me as I declare His glory. My path then will open before me and I will move through into the land God is calling me to possess and occupy. I declare that the new vision of the future is coming alive in me, with my shout will come divine light that will illuminate my path. Shout – Lord create the new – Lord I align with your executive counsel and enter into new lands, jobs, creative adventures and the next level of divine promise for my life, I am released from the old identity of the past, I am aligned with God for my future. I am going forward to overcome. I cut ties with every familiar spirit of immorality and every thing that will defile my land and declare an end to covenant breaking in my land. My life will rejoice and the Lord will bring the power of restoration to work in my life, whatever has been stolen from me in the past is restored seven fold in this next season in Jesus name. I declare that Heaven and Earth will connect and a new and higher level of communication with God will begin in my life. I declare today that my life will begin to produce in a new way such that my storehouses will become full. I declare a season of rest in my life. Every reproach of the past, every failure and disappointment, every unbelief from the past that is connected with my life, my inheritance and future is rolled away from me today; God will break open wells of salvation in my life and renew my spirit. I receive a spirit of revelation, I see angelic host around me helping me, ascending and descending to bring me help. The Holy Spirit is filling my life anew and afresh.

WARRIORS UNDERSTAND SPIRITUAL TIMING

*"So teach us to number our days,
That we may gain a heart of wisdom."
Psalm 90:12 NKJV*

This scripture challenges us to number our days according to God's wisdom not the wisdom of this world or the satanic wisdom that amounts to nothing. The warrior knows how to make time a friend, it is great wisdom to understand time and part of the warrior's mindset knows how to use time. A warrior understands that time affects every aspect of life and that our success depends on how we understand and cooperate with the timings of God.

David and Joseph were two warriors in the Bible who

understood God's timing. When David was first anointed in 1 Samuel 16, he was a teenager, a few years later he was anointed over Judah in 2 Samuel 2:1-2 but it was not until after seven years and six months of war with house of Saul in 2 Samuel 5:1-5 that he was eventually anointed as king of the whole nation of Israel. It took almost thirteen years for God's word to come to pass in his life but throughout that time he stayed in a warrior's mode and mindset. The same can be said for Joseph.

> *"Until the time that his word came to pass,*
> *The word of the LORD tested him."*
> *Psalm 105:19 NKJV*

Joseph and David passed the test of time

There are other examples of people who failed the test of time. Uzziah was such an example; he had a very brilliant start in 2 Chronicles 26:1-16 but such a terrible finish as a leper. He was helped so marvelously that he soon forgot who was helping him and missed God along the way. Pride is the greatest trap for the warrior; the warrior knows that whoever succeeds in escaping the subtle trap of pride will make it to the end.

There was another king in Israel called Manasseh who recovered just in time from the poison of pride in a most significant way. He was a man comparable to Gaddafi, Stalin, Hitler, Saddam, Sanni Abacha of Nigeria, or Assad of Syria. He was a bloody king ready to kill anyone opposed to him; he was also wicked and rebellious against God. Manasseh had a godly father and mother but chose to reject God from an early age; he directly opposed God and even worshipped idols inside God's temple just to show how much he didn't care. He wanted to hear nothing from God and he was reputed to have killed the prophet Isaiah by sawing him into two halves between wooden planks. This is why it seems inconceivable that when this extremely wicked man repented, God forgave him and restored him. [2 Chronicles 33:10-16]

Manasseh's pride was broken excruciatingly when he was conquered and subjected to some of the treatment he had levied to others. He was not only humbled by the circumstances, but he was smart enough to humble himself deeply before God. In the case of Uzziah it was his pride that killed him. It was also true of Saul the first king of Israel; it was pride that cost him his life and crown. Manasseh however found restoration through repentance and forgiveness. Joseph was not a proud man at all, he was the humblest of men, and no state or position changed him as a person or affected his communion and relationship with God. David too did not have the root of pride in him; in spite of his struggles and all he had to endure as Saul hunted him over several years, he made it to the throne. Pride is the key factor that can make you lose timing with God. You must understand that one of the greatest battles you will ever fight is against pride. Christ came to restore among other things your ability to perceive and regain the correct timings of God. When your spirit is tuned to obey God, you will walk with patience and humility. Pride is associated with lust, anger and impatience with resultant loss. For instance when Uzziah was challenged for doing wrong, his response was anger,
"… He was wroth …" [2 Chronicles 26:19]

The warrior understands patience and the power of endurance.

> *"For when God made a promise to Abraham, because He could swear by no one greater, He swore by Himself, saying, "Surely blessing I will bless you, and multiplying I will multiply you. And so, after he had patiently endured, he obtained the promise."*
> *Hebrews 6:13-15 NKJV*

But Abraham had to patiently endure; he had a warrior's heart. If you know where you are going, you will not be upset with where you are. The life of Jesus was also one of vision and timing. Things may not be working as you want it but if you can stay excited about your tomorrow, then your change will surely come. When you understand Godly timing it will produce courage, boldness, security and strength. A wise man's heart is associated with discerning time and judgment … It takes discipline to wait for God, because although God is never late, many people grow weary not because God is delaying His promise or answer to prayer, but because they are not in tune with God. Pride is a major attitude that turns God off, but if you are not full of pride, it's never too late with God. If God can forgive Manasseh when he repented, you can turn around right now and God will give you a new beginning. [Ecclesiastes 8:5]

There are five keys that will help you to walk in Spiritual timing. The first is spiritual hunger, when there is hunger for more of God; it will provoke God to change your season. Spiritual hunger is what will cause your heart to align with God's purpose, this is why and how fasting works. Fasting doesn't change God but your hunger will change you and position you to receive from God. [Matthew 5:8; Isaiah 44:3]

One of the offshoots of hunger is the grace for enquiry, a thirst to know the answers to often perturbing spiritual questions and to ask with confidence knowing that when you ask, you shall receive an answer. [Matthew 7:7; James 1:5] Sometimes God will put people around you, matured believers who can counsel and advice you about right timing. [2 Samuel 5:18-19, 23-24; Jeremiah 6:16] The third thing hunger will provoke is sensitivity to divine timing. [John 11:1-11; Luke 1:80] Hunger will also help us submit to godly authority; always remember that submission is designed for our protection and spiritual covering. [Esther 2:10] The big final key is actually a commandment that says if you will walk in God's timing and keep your motives pure, you will see God, "... The pure in heart shall see God ... " [Matthew 5:8]

"When I would have healed Israel, Then the iniquity of Ephraim was uncovered,
And the wickedness of Samaria. For they have committed fraud; A thief comes in;
A band of robbers takes spoil outside.
Hosea 7:1 NKJV

God is always for you. He wants to release the Sword of the Spirit through your mouth to release your future and walk in perfect timing with you. But you must prepare yourself for change and declare total war against the devil for your time of restoration. I declare that as you read this book and the Holy Spirit stirs your heart God will remember you. May this become for you a season of divine remembrance where you will see Jesus in a new way. Maybe you already know Him as Saviour and have known Him as the Good Shepherd but I pray that in these pages you will encounter Him as Captain and Warrior King.

> *"The LORD shall go forth like a mighty man; He shall stir up His zeal like a man of war.*
> *He shall cry out, yes, shout aloud; He shall prevail against His enemies. I have held My peace a long time, I have been still and restrained Myself. Now I will cry like a woman in labor, I will pant and gasp at once. I will lay waste the mountains and hills, And dry up all their vegetation; I will make the rivers coastlands, And I will dry up the pools. I will bring the blind by a way they did not know; I will lead them in paths they have not known. I will make darkness light before them, And crooked places straight. These things I will do for them, And not forsake them."*
> *Isaiah 42:13-16 NKJV*

The Lord has sworn to lead you and bless you in His own divine timing but you must not conform to the world. Conformity to the world will only delay God's timing and purpose. The only one who knows who you can become is your creator. The world is peddling sin; television and other media constantly glamorize and advertise sin and immorality. While the voice of the world around you urge you to follow after sin and tries to convince you that you are missing the fun, the word of God says don't conform. God says don't conform because He wants to deliver His best into your life.

> *"I beseech you therefore, brethren, by the mercies of God, that you present your bodies a living sacrifice, holy, acceptable to God, which is your reasonable service. And do not be conformed to this world, but be transformed by the renewing of your mind, that you may prove what is that good and acceptable and perfect will of God."*
> *Romans 12:1-2 NKJV*

As long as you are in a world that is sold out on promoting and propagating pleasures of the flesh, the battle will continue to rage between your flesh and your spirit, it is only as you expose yourself to God and practice godliness that you will disarm the powers of sin and compromise.

> *"For the flesh lusts against the Spirit, and the Spirit against the flesh; and these are contrary to one another, so that you do not do the things that you wish."*
> Galatians 5:17 NKJV

Many people find it easier to yield to the things around them because that is the simplest thing to do, watch some more TV, read magazines, eat a little bit more, so it is easier to walk in the flesh than it is to walk in the spirit. But when we begin to spend more time with God, it becomes easy to follow the Holy Spirit. Draw near to God consciously, deliberately and consistently and you will begin to discern His timing.

> *"Therefore do not let sin reign in your mortal body, that you should obey it in its lusts. And do not present your members as instruments of unrighteousness to sin, but present yourselves to God as being alive from the dead, and your members as instruments of righteousness to God. For sin shall not have dominion over you, for you are not under law but under grace."*
> Romans 6:12-14 NKJV

> *"I speak in human terms because of the weakness of your flesh. For just as you presented your members as slaves of uncleanness, and of lawlessness leading to more lawlessness, so now present your members as slaves of righteousness for holiness."*
> Romans 6:19 NKJV

In the race for righteousness, you must keep examining yourself and asking, "Who am I becoming?" You will always be the crucial and determining factor in reaching your destination with God in God's time not the devil. Sin will always remain at the root of human calamity. Until you destroy the roots of sin, you will keep seeing its fruits. If you are not born again you have a death sentence hanging on your head and it is just a matter of time before it is executed.

> *"And you, being dead in your trespasses and the uncircumcision of your flesh, He has made alive together with Him, having forgiven you all trespasses, having wiped out the handwriting of requirements that was against us, which was contrary to us. And He has taken it out of the way, having nailed it to the cross."*
> Colossians 2:13-14 NKJV

If you have given your life to Jesus the sentence of death is revoked and the handwriting contrary to you is blotted out; but just as salvation signifies the forgiveness of sins and a quickening unto righteousness, it is important to note that it is only the beginning of a journey of restoration. The message of Jesus is clear, when you become born again; you become a spirit in the likeness of God although you are still living in a natural body. This body is not yet saved. It does not change with salvation and so will still demand to practice the old things. But the message of the gospel says that while you are still in this body and living in a world that is going in the opposite direction you can look like God and act like God by yielding to the Holy Spirit.

> *"That which is born of the flesh is flesh, and that which is born of the Spirit is spirit."*
> John 3:6 NKJV

Every blessing takes its root from the Holy Spirit; the Holy Spirit will never lead you into unrighteousness and so the blessings of divine remembrance flow from righteousness.

When Jesus abides in your life, every other blessing will come and overtake you.

One of the cheapest ways to provoke divine remembrance is to reason your way out of unrighteousness. When you are saved, your mind can be transformed by God's word to enable you to reason with God.

> *"Come now, and let us reason together,"*
> *Says the LORD,*
> *"Though your sins are like scarlet,*
> *They shall be as white as snow;*
> *Though they are red like crimson,*
> *They shall be as wool."*
> *Isaiah 1:18 NKJV*

Correct thinking is what establishes a correct turning around. Ask yourself, "What do I benefit from this thing, what has it ever offered anyone?" You cannot think straight and live crooked. If you can think straight you will live straight. Start to reason with God, this is the key to restoration.

> *"Now therefore, thus says the LORD of hosts: "Consider your ways!"*
> *Haggai 1:5 NKJV*

To walk in divine timing the warrior understands the need to exercise herself or himself in holiness. Holiness is what provokes divine remembrance but holiness is like a spiritual sport, it requires exercise and diligence. Christianity is described as a race, just as in every sport; exercise is the rule of championship. In the same way, a Christian must exercise restraint against every kind of unrighteousness.

"This being so, I myself always strive to have a conscience without

> *offense toward God and men."*
> *Acts 24:16 NKJV*

> *"But reject profane and old wives' fables, and exercise yourself toward godliness. For bodily exercise profits a little, but godliness is profitable for all things, having promise of the life that now is and of that which is to come."*
> *1 Timothy 4:7-8 NKJV*

Sin and unrighteousness are not friends, they destroy, when in your lives, they make God look away from you and you loose divine timing. The media glamorizes sin but it is poison to the spirit. Godliness that retains the presence of God requires continuous spiritual exercise to be enforced.

> *"You therefore must endurefn hardship as a good soldier of Jesus Christ. No one engaged in warfare entangles himself with the affairs of this life, that he may please him who enlisted him as a soldier. And also if anyone competes in athletics, he is not crowned unless he competes according to the rules."*
> *2 Timothy 2:3-5 NKJV*

Paul tells us here that your body can be subject to the power of your will when it is hooked up to the grace of God. If you lack the focus and determination, you can frustrate the grace of God. But there's help available to position you under the loving gaze of the Almighty, that help can empower you to say no to immorality, to corruption, to bitterness, envy, strife, lying and cheating.

> *Nothing happens in your life without your permission. Begin to say no to hell and its suggestions and yes to practical holiness.*
> *Declare,*
> *"my season of restoration is now!"*

> *"Beloved, now we are children of God; and it has not yet been revealed what we shall be, but we know that when He is revealed, we shall be like Him, for we shall see Him as He is. And everyone who has this hope in Him purifies himself, just as He is pure."*
> 1 John 3:2-3 NKJV

Don't wait for anyone to come and do it for you. You must take up the responsibility to purify yourself. Godly exercises are the only pathway to a dignified Christian life.

Receive strength in jesus name to watch and pray. To watch implies to exercise. If the consequences of sin are so horrible here, imagine what hell will be like. If you are sleeping in the wrong bed get out now, or if you are in a shady business for quick money, stop it now!

> *"Now the Spirit expressly says that in latter times some will depart from the faith, giving heed to deceiving spirits and doctrines of demons, speaking lies in hypocrisy, having their own conscience seared with a hot iron,"*
> 1 Timothy 4:1-2 NKJV

You must listen to your conscience to walk in divine timing. Seducing spirits can silence the voice of the conscience. The fact that everyone is doing it doesn't matter, and you may even think it is not a sin it is only natural. But your conscience is the scale of justice, it will tell you what is wrong. Don't kill your conscience with seducing spirits. God is planning a glorious time for you but Satan is planning perilous times.

> *"But know this, that in the last days perilous times will come:"*
> 2 Timothy 3:1 NKJV

You always have the power of choice. Daniel and Joseph in the Bible were able to resist great temptation at a time when the Holy Spirit was not within because they made a choice to draw near to God. They obviously got close enough to God to fight and win the battle over the flesh.

"But Daniel purposed in his heart that he would not defile himself with the portion of the king's delicacies, nor with the wine which he drank; therefore he requested of the chief of the eunuchs that he might not defile himself."
Daniel 1:8 NKJV

" And it came to pass after these things that his master's wife cast longing eyes on Joseph, and she said, "Lie with me." But he refused and said to his master's wife, "Look, my master does not know what is with me in the house, and he has committed all that he has to my hand. "There is no one greater in this house than I, nor has he kept back anything from me but you, because you are his wife. How then can I do this great wickedness, and sin against God?" Genesis 39:7-9 NKJV

" Come out from among them And be separate, says the Lord. Do not touch what is unclean,
And I will receive you. I will be a Father to you, And you shall be My sons and daughters,
Says the LORD Almighty." 2 Corinthians 6:17-18 NKJV

Chose to come out of sin, don't just try. Come out of immorality, lying, financial corruption, deception, and craftiness. Choose to be straight. Initially it may look like you are in prison like Joseph, but as you walk with God, the God who remembered Joseph would also remember you and they will send for you. This is your hour of deliverance so begin to purpose in your heart to lay aside every sin and every weight. You can stop that habit now before it stops you. Satan is not fully responsible for what happens in your life; sin has no power of dominion over you. The moment you disconnect, that tree of evil will be uprooted in your life. The communion table is a powerful ordinance for breaking soul ties and habits that hinder you from godliness. Call that stubborn sin or habit by name and disconnect with it now at the Table of the Lord. God did not plant sin or sickness to plague your life so disconnect from it now in Jesus name.

Communion Scriptures

John 6:54-57
"Whoever eats My flesh and drinks My blood has eternal life, and I will raise him up at the last day. For My flesh is food indeed, and My blood is drink indeed. He who eats My flesh and drinks My blood abides in Me, and I in him. As the living Father sent Me, and I live because of the Father, so he who feeds on Me will live because of Me."
NKJV

1 Corinthians 11:23-25
"For I received from the Lord that which I also delivered to you: that the Lord Jesus on the same night in which He was betrayed took bread; and when He had given thanks, He broke it and said, "Take, eat; this is My body which is broken for you; do this in remembrance of Me." In the same manner He also took the cup after supper, saying, "This cup is the new covenant in My blood. This do, as often as you drink it, in remembrance of Me."
NKJV

1 Corinthians 5:7-8
" Therefore purge out the old leaven, that you may be a new lump,

since you truly are unleavened. For indeed Christ, our Passover, was sacrificed for us Therefore let us keep the feast, not with old leaven, nor with the leaven of malice and wickedness, but with the unleavened bread of sincerity and truth."
NKJV

Ephesians 1:7
"In Him we have redemption through His blood, the forgiveness of sins, according to the riches of His grace"
NKJV

Romans 5: 9
"Much more then, having now been justified by His blood, we shall be saved from wrath through Him. "
NKJV

Exodus 12:13
"Now the blood shall be a sign for you on the houses where you are. And when I see the blood, I will pass over you; and the plague shall not be on you to destroy you when I strike the land of Egypt."
NKJV

Zechariah 9:11-12
"As for you also, Because of the blood of your covenant, I will set your prisoners free from the waterless pit. Return to the stronghold,
You prisoners of hope. Even today I declare That I will restore double to you. "
NKJV

Hebrews 9:14
"How much more shall the blood of Christ, who through the eternal Spirit offered Himself without spot to God, cleanse your conscience from dead works to serve the living God?"
NKJV

This is the hour of liberty and the blood is the answer to the strongest hold of sin, it has access to purge your conscience, it can quicken and bring things back to life, there is power in the blood. When your conscience is clear you have greater access to God's voice and spiritual timing.

Confessions:

I have power by the Blood of Jesus to make every pharaoh in my life to bow, I declare that all the enemies of my life and future must bow and submit to the Spirit of God at work in me. By the Blood of Jesus I enter into riches and honour; the same way Israel spoiled Egypt in the days of exodus, I shall spoil my captors and enemies of my soul. I bind myself to the wisdom of God. I receive the wisdom of God that showed them the way to go and from today I enter into restoration for my life and declare I shall not be stranded anymore. As Israel journeyed, none was feeble in their tribe and so I declare that the Blood of Jesus turns every weakness in my life to strength. No more sickness and no more shame in my way. Failure, disappointment and shame have come to an end from today. I am curse free because my God has remembered me. I am blessed and highly favoured because the blood of Jesus is speaking for me.

Heavenly Father, forgive me for all the areas of my life I have not yielded to you. Forgive me for compromises that I have made and grant me courage to pull down all the strongholds of deception that I have defended through ignorance. I bind myself to the truth of the gospel of Jesus Christ and reject every falsehood and deception in Jesus name. By the power of the Holy Spirit I resist every work of Satan and the influences that makes me compromise with sin and those things that would throw me out of spiritual timing for my life. I declare I will walk in divine alignment with God's purpose for my life. I submit myself to the Holy Spirit of truth and ask that the light of God's countenance in the name of Jesus Christ would expose every sin and self-deception in my life.

I receive a sound mind and grace for a consistent walk with God. I declare that every frustration, barrenness, sickness, failure, confusion and stagnation comes to an end in my life. I declare I will never be late but will walk in divine alignment with God. I see heaven begin to react against every obstacle in my way. The pathway of disappointment ends in my life today and I declare the peace of God like a river flows into my life. God is building me up as a warrior and equipping me to march forward into my future. I release into my life the grace for covenant timing in the name of Jesus; I declare it is time for my long awaited miracle that will make my testimony complete in Jesus name.

WARRIORS FIGHT THE FIGHT OF FAITH

"Yet in all these things we are more than conquerors through Him who loved us."
Romans 8:37 NKJV

Life demands that we contest to conquer. It is part of God's divine program for man to have opposition and challenges, but God also designed us to overcome every obstacle and make every challenge a stepping-stone to upward change. No challenge or discouragement should be strong enough to discourage us from following the plans of God. [Mark 5:25-34; 10:46-52]

Challenges are part of the arrangement if you are to posses your inheritance. God will not cut corners for you in your assignment. If you see no challenges you will see no victory. Every challenge is an attack on your confidence. Satan knows that when confidence suffers, courage is lost. Without courage you cannot possess your inheritance. When Israel was delivered from the bondage of slavery in Egypt, God knew that war was part of the programme but they were not yet ready so He took them through a longer way to enable them get ready.

> *"Then it came to pass, when Pharaoh had let the people go, that God did not lead them by way of the land of the Philistines, although that was near; for God said, "Lest perhaps the people change their minds when they see war, and return to Egypt."*
> *Exodus 13:17 NKJV*

Every challenge and opposition is initiated and planned by the devil. He may use people; believers or unbelievers and he may use deliberate temptations like hunger or lust. This is why you must never take anyone to heart face as your enemy but learn how to fight the main culprit, the devil (2 Corinthians 10:3). It is neither wise nor profitable to react to challenges in the flesh, the warrior learns how to discern and respond in the spirit. Your challenges and the opposition that rises against you is not an affliction, so don't feel depressed or dejected; see it as a sign of promotion because if Satan is not bothered about you then possibly you are already a failure. Challenges and opposition are mostly an indication that your star is rising up. Remember that opposition is often a tool of distraction.

Distraction is what makes you major on minor issues. Every challenge is meant to distract you; if the enemy cannot derail you, he will try to delay you. If your focus is steered off course long enough it might become your destination. If you refuse to fear when you are challenged, you will be able to think more clearly to find a solution.

"But none of these things move me; nor do I count my life dear to myself, so that I may finish my race with joy, and the ministry which I received from the Lord Jesus, to testify to the gospel of the grace of God." Acts 20:24 NKJV

Be not afraid; if you do not want to suffer then refuse to submit to fear. Fear is the first and strongest foothold of Satan in any life. The blind beggar and the woman with the issue of blood in the Gospel of Mark overcame their fear before they could release their faith and receive their miracle. The way to remain ahead in victory and not turn tail in defeat is to be full of faith. We are required to fight the good fight of faith. It is a fight to overcome our fears. Fear breeds confusion and instability because it works with other spirits to put people in bondage. Fear works with other spirits like poverty and sickness. The spirit of poverty says God is not able to handle what is ahead for me, fear works with sickness to weaken your ability to stand, fear will also work with anger so that you react in anger instead of embracing change that is required to move ahead. We must also understand that fear can be either an emotion or a demonic spirit.

> *"For God has not given us a spirit of fear, but of power and of love and of a sound mind."*
> *2 Timothy 1:7 NKJV*

The Bible clearly calls fear a spirit, but fear is also a powerful unpleasant feeling associated with risks or danger and this emotion can be real or imagined. Biologically it is a defensive response to a stimulus that has entered the atmosphere around us. Many of us have heard of the 3F's - fight, faint or flee. Fear is often based on something you think may happen in the future and when you begin to create a scenario in your mind that is not based on what God has said it creates friction and vexation in your soul and may result in weakness or infirmity.

The warrior's mindset obeys God's commandment to Joshua to be courageous, the warrior embraces the courage required to overcome fear because of the realization that there is no promised land without giants. Our nature as Christians should be one of boldness. What then shall we say to these things? If God is for us, who can be against us? (Romans 8:31) Boldness is an emotion that must be stirred up and it is only scriptural knowledge that can stir up boldness. The consciousness of right standing with God is what instills boldness and courage. [Colossians 1:9-13; Ephesians 3:16-20; Isaiah 54:11-17]

The warrior understands that every time the enemy reminds you of past mistakes, it is to make you lose strength; he wants you to feel unworthy. Satan knows that how you feel will affect your faith. Therefore cheer up and understand that God is not holding your faults against you, He says come to me with boldness to my throne of grace and you will meet with my mercy and find grace sufficient for your need. To remain bold you must always remind yourself of the love of God. [Hebrews4: 16; Jude 20-22]

Keep Matching Forward in Faith

"Examine yourselves as to whether you are in the faith. Test yourselves. Do you not know yourselves that Jesus Christ is in you? —unless indeed you are disqualified."
2 Corinthians 13:5 NKJV

Self-examination is possibly the first sign of Christian maturity. The grace to submit to the scrutiny of conscience and the Holy Spirit and ask God to search you out is the beginning of true humility. It is the beginning of a holy life. You must be ready to stand in the place of personal examination. As long as a person doesn't know that he doesn't know, he never grows.

> *"To be conscious that you are ignorant of the fact is a great help to knowledge"*
> *Benjamin Disraeli*

One of the things to check up during consistent self examination, is to be sure you are going where you want to go, otherwise challenges and situations of life may start determining where to go. It is important to continuously examine, define and refocus your life vision and let that dictate both the momentum and direction of your life. There must be something you are living for. Someone once said, 'If you don't know what to live for you won't know what to run from.'

For the warrior, it is the vision of the future that provides great motivation and the energy that drives toward success and to overcome challenges. It is a product of both the mind and imagination. The warrior will constantly engage the mind and imagination to fashion a great tomorrow because a future you cannot imagine, you may never experience. Through a purified imagination you can project into the future and into God's counsel for your life, this is the great principle of the Holy Scriptures. [Genesis 13:14-15; Genesis 15:5-6]

God stimulated Abraham's imagination with such illustrations that he had no choice but to continuously focus on God's promise through his imagination despite his personal challenges. Your imagination will play a pivotal role in overcoming challenges and entering into the destiny of greatness that God has prepared for you. Imagination has the ability to draw to you the things you imagine. Imagination creates a vision and expectation; expectation will generate enthusiasm and enthusiasm will always dismantle opposition and challenges through motion.

A warrior is a believer who is wholesome in spirit and mind; sometimes God wants to take over your imagination so that the Holy Spirit can think through you. As we grow in the Lord, we may initiate the thinking but as we think, God plants His ideas and programme's into our minds. [Matthew 1:20]

Personal responsibility is required to cultivate the solitude required to think in the frequency of the Holy Spirit. Many things will seek your attention but only one thing is needful, that is your vision or assignment. How bright you can keep your vision in focus will determine the speed of your accomplishment. As I stated earlier, the warrior spirit is indefatigable and through meditation and focus, the heart is prepared for one purpose only – pursuit. The warrior's strategy is to keep at it. Keep at your job, pursuit or vision - whatever you are doing is affecting the devil so do it more. [Luke 9:62]

Anywhere you see the enemy attacking means you must succeed in that area. Just refuse to stop. Examine the progress of the first church - (Acts 4:4 - five thousand saved; Acts 4:16 - they were challenged and threatened; Acts 4:31 - they prayed for boldness; Acts 5:17-18 - they were imprisoned; Acts 5:19-20 - God said do more Acts 6:7 – the result and testimony of their persistence)

Walk in Love

"For in Christ Jesus neither circumcision nor un-circumcision avails anything, but faith working through love."
Galatians 5:6

Nothing works without love because faith is everything. Satan may use people to provoke you to hatred and bitterness but your depth of love will eventually determine your height in life. Be determined to be a repairer not a destroyer, we are to be builders of the body not bulldozers.

" Blessed are you when they revile and persecute you, and say all kinds of evil against you falsely for My sake."
Matthew 5:11 NKJV

True love will always involve sacrifice, no matter what anyone does to abuse or humiliate you; you must work towards that persons highest good. However, the Bible is clear that we do not war against flesh and blood and so even when people have been used to provoke you or stand against you, be aware the real enemy is Satan and you need to launch a spiritual counter-attack. The warrior understands the importance of counter-attack.

But He said to them, " But He said to them, "Why are you fearful, O you of little faith?" Then He arose and rebuked the winds and the sea, and there was a great calm." Matthew 8:26 NKJV

Behind every opposition is a spiritual storm, address it. When Jesus addressed the storm, it obeyed Him. When you sense opposition building up against you begin to act boldly in the ordinances against Satan and then have faith for signs and wonders. Believe the impossible; believe in the supernatural help of God. [Hebrews 12:12-15; Mark 16:17; Acts 2:22]

Expect a miracle as God's seal of approval. When challenges and oppositions arise make sure you progress until your progress silences the protest of challengers. You must believe that you are destined to succeed.

Do Not Be Passive - Case Study: David

> *"To the Chief Musician. A Psalm of David the servant of the LORD, who spoke to the LORD the words of this song on the day that the LORD delivered him from the hand of all his enemies and from the hand of Saul. And he said: I will love You, O LORD, my strength. he LORD is my rock and my fortress and my deliverer; My God, my strength, in whom I will trust; My shield and the horn of my salvation, my stronghold."*
> *Psalm 18:1-2 NKJV*

The introduction to this psalm tells us David expressed these words in the day that God had delivered him from the hand of all his enemies and the hand of Saul. The entire psalm is also found repeated in 2 Samuel 22. It is a careful summary of David's character, his relationship with God and an attitude of life he maintained. David testified several times in the Psalms how God had delivered him out of the hands of all his enemies. That tells me that there is a place in God where you can have total deliverance; where He sets a table before you in the presence of your enemies and gives you victory over every challenge. Even though the enemies are there, enemies no longer matter in the presence of God. A day came in the life of David and he penned this psalm because God Almighty had delivered Him out of the hands of all his enemies. I pray that this year, the same Almighty God will deliver you from all your enemies, both internal and external. I pray that God will grant you freedom from all spiritual forces that hinder your progress. I pray that God will bring you to a place where you will write and sing a new song of deliverance. May The Lord God give you a song of victory in the name of Jesus Christ.

David's song demonstrates his absolute conviction in the absolute power and authority of Jehovah and His mighty ability to deliver. It also demonstrates David's understanding that obedience is very important to God, that obedience to God's law is one of the greatest assurances of God's intervention. David had a warrior's mentality.

What David expresses in the psalm was an experience born out of relationship with God, he could relate directly to the God who delivered him from Goliath, protected him from Saul, from Israel's enemies, from his son Absalom and from his own sinful passions. As a warrior he uses military symbols to describe God:

1. A ROCK that cannot be penetrated by the enemy
2. A FORTRESS a place of security where the enemy cannot follow
3. A BUCKLER/SHIELD that comes between him and harm
4. A HORN OF SALVATION a symbol of might and power
5. A TOWER high above all his enemies

Interestingly enough, David was not a fighter by nature, he was a worshipper who wanted to be in God's presence more than he wanted to fight anybody, but as soon as he was anointed everybody wanted to fight him. David personally experienced God in all these different ways expressed by this psalm. Even when enemies surrounded him, he sought to know God more, and was willing for God to teach him to fight.

> *"For who is God, except the LORD? And who is a rock, except our God? It is God who arms me with strength, And makes my way perfect. He makes my feet like the feet of deer, And sets me on my high places. He teaches my hands to make war, So that my arms can bend a bow of bronze. You have also given me the shield of Your salvation; Your right hand has held me up, Your gentleness has made me great."*
> Psalm 18:31-35 NKJV

But the more David worshipped God and the more he entered into the presence of God, the more enemies rose up against him and the more he needed God to teach him how to fight and be victorious. Each time David was anointed and recognised, enemies rose up against him. This is still very true today; the anointing on your life will attract opposition because the purpose of the anointing is to enable you stand against something or do something for God. Jesus in Matthew 10:1 gave his disciples power to stand against unclean spirits. The bible speaking of Jesus says,

> *"You love righteousness and hate wickedness; Therefore God, Your God, has anointed You With the oil of gladness more than Your companions."*
> Psalm 45:7 NKJV

God will only anoint you to the degree that you hate wickedness and you love righteousness. And so when you are anointed, it is an enablement from God to stand for Him and against what He is opposed to. If you stand against nothing, you stand in a dangerous place because things will surely come against you. If you are not pushing you will soon be pushed out of the way. As soon as David was anointed, he was challenged with the Goliath situation to see if indeed he believed in what he had received. This song demonstrates David's absolute trust in God's absolute might and power to deliver and set free. His trust was entirely in God. His confidence was totally in God. It also shows that David understood the power of obedience in his relationship with God. He understood that he could only connect with God's saving power through his obedience to God's love and law. God is not someone we can manipulate and control. God is the Almighty that we submit to and through our submission we become one with Him. David understood that. What David was exalting in Psalm 18:2 were expressions that described God in military terms. These were all military symbols and as you study you find that they were also names that describe Jesus Christ. What David was extolling was based on his experience of God. They were inspired from an intimate relationship with God and walk with God. This was the man who fought Goliath and won, who ran from Saul and overcame Saul as an enemy. He was a man who was challenged by his own son Absalom but escaped the wrath and conspiracy of Absalom. He was a man who fought all Israel's battles and won. He was a man who also fought his own passion and lust. David fought many battles but he came to recognize God as the one who saw him through it all.

David called God a rock. What did he mean by a rock? A rock stands for something that cannot be penetrated by the enemy. God was to David a rock that cannot be penetrated. He also called God a fortress. A fortress is a place of security where the enemy cannot follow; it is also a place where the enemy can be trapped and destroyed. David saw God as his fortress. When you begin to understand David's mind and his concept and his image of God then you will understand his confidence in God. You will understand how this young man as a teenager could march forward into the battlefield to face Goliath.

From the very beginning of this song, David praised the image of God in his heart and revealed God, as he knew Him. We must admit that it is possible to be a Christian for a long time and have an image of God in your heart that is incompatible with the God in the Holy Scriptures. This is why your mind must be renewed by God's word to have the proper image of who God really is. These metaphors of David describe his experience of God. They were not just images from his mind. They were descriptions of the reality of his walk, realities of battles he had fought and won. He saw God as rock. There were times in his life when he saw God as the only barrier between him and the enemy. There were times in his life he had to run into hiding knowing that the enemy could not penetrate.

David saw God as his 'Buckler and Shield'. These were instruments of war that comes between a warrior and harm. In David's mind he understood that for harm to reach him, it would have to go through God first. No wonder he never lost a battle and was always courageous. Indeed, as a man thinks in his heart so is he. This is why the Bible is emphatic about the renewal of the mind. Out of your heart will proceed every issue of your life and so, when your mind is renewed by the word and promises of God, blessings begin to flow into your life. This song by David is a testimony of the things flowing from David's heart. He saw standing between him and Goliath the God who was his armour and shield. The shield of Goliath weighed more than David but in David's heart he saw a metal shield that was nothing compared to God, his own unseen shield and buckler. That was the image in David's mind. And I tell you when you begin to see God in this realm you won't be afraid.

David saw God as his horn of salvation. The horn is always regarded as a symbol of strength and power. He saw God as his high tower that rises far above all his enemies. Although David was a man surrounded by many adversaries throughout his life and though he was not perfect in many ways, the fact that he sought God more than anything else distinguished him. The more he came under pressure, the more he pressed into God. This is perhaps the greatest lesson we can learn from David and this is one of the challenges we must overcome as Christians. Where do you turn to when the challenges mount up? For many people what shakes them off from God is that trial. When tests and tribulations spring up many forget about clinging to God but cling to the problem and call it "my problem". David was not like that. David was a worshipper. And so when things came against him he sought God and worshipped because he trusted that God was in control of his life. Most of the psalms were penned as David sought God and craved for a closer relationship. He understood that if he could just get closer to God, the problem will move away or get solved in God's presence where fullness of joy is promised. He knew that the deeper I get into God's presence the further I am from the problem.

Everyone will encounter challenging issues; they are part of life. Challenges are part of the territory but when challenges come and you focus too much on it that you lose focus on God, you create a bigger challenge. Sometimes we deceive ourselves by claiming our focus is on prayer but when we pray in fear or by rote without any shred of faith in God's unfailing love, it may be a wasted effort. Without faith we cannot please God and God is a God of knowledge by whom actions are weighed. Praying and fasting about an issue is not wrong, we should just be careful we don't become totally dominated by the problem until we can't see any other thing. God said, "Draw near to me." In drawing near sometimes all we need to do is worship Him. Leave that problem alone. The bible says, "He knows you have need of these things already." There is nothing that you are going through that God doesn't already know. Sometimes all the grace we need is to leave the issue aside and come to God. If only you can imagine David in Psalm 3, when he was running from his son Absalom who had just disgraced him and who sought to kill him. David slept and woke up that morning in the wilderness, he had just left his palace and throne and the comfort of his wives and servants. But he woke up to worship God in spite of his circumstances, he woke up in the wilderness not to complain or gripe against God but to worship and find God worthy of thanksgiving. He said in essence, I worship you because I could sleep and wake up, I acknowledge that even in my sleeping and waking you sustained me. You are the glory and the lifter up of my head. David understood God enough to know that you don't get to God or get the best from Him by complaining about what is happening or has happened. If I must get his attention, I must start with thanksgiving. David must have searched around him for what he could thank God for. There was nothing thankworthy around David except that he was alive. Shimei had just insulted him the previous day splashing him with mud and cursing at him. But David's response was sober and with great humility, his thoughts were something like this. 'I understand that nobody can deliver me from this situation. I also understand that God has protocol in place. To gain the access required for my deliverance and restoration I must enter His presence with thanksgiving.'

Therefore he looked around and must have reasoned. 'Is there nothing I can thank God for in this situation? I've been chased out of Jerusalem, my throne has been taken, I have been humiliated by my subjects and disgraced by my son but at least I woke up. I slept and I woke up." That was the first key to David's total recovery. And so he began from there, as long as he could find praise he regained his ground. In every situation, when you find the heart to praise God, you are on your way to recovery.

Reject Apathy/Passivity

Although David was a worshipper and lover of God by nature, he allowed God to teach him how to fight. God had to teach him how to fight (verse 32 and 35). We must ask God to teach us how to fight. David inquired of God to lead and guide him in every situation because he trusted in God more than his experience as a warrior. Until God taught him to fight he could not overcome his enemies. God also taught David not to be passive. God taught David not to live in apathy. God taught David to be proactive.

To be passive is to be inactive; it is to be non-participating in the issues of life. Some people in an organization or fellowship want to warm the benches, just sit in the background and remain inactive. They choose not to participate. One of the things God taught David is not to be a passive person spiritually. Don't be passive in your spirit. This means being unresisting but receptive and submitting to external forces. Passive people are unresisting to the devil. External forces easily control them. The only person they don't hear from is God. They hear every rumour about everything else except what God is saying. They can tell you what is the latest in the news but ask them, "What has God said?" and they have no idea. One of the things God taught David was to reject apathy and refuse to be passive.

> *Passivity has its origin from Latin "passivus" meaning - susceptible to suffering!*

This was the state in which Israel found themselves in 1 Samuel 17 when the entire army had died forty times or imagined death at the hands of Goliath for forty consecutive days. When David arrived at the battlefield, he went for a different reason but discovered another mission from God. This is one of the profound mysteries of God worth noting. David was under the authority of his earthly father and was on an errand of obedience to his earthly father when he encountered God's higher purpose. The implication is that if someone cannot be faithful in simple tasks in the house of God yet they want big assignments from God, they will wait a long time. David was open; he was a servant at heart, he was content to remain with sheep when the great prophet of God was visiting and he was happy to take food on a donkey to the battlefront for his brothers.

> *The reality in God is that often it is only as we submit to authority do we discover God's higher purpose for us beyond the natural.*

This is why it takes submission to have access to authority. Many times God will put someone in your life on earth physically that you need to submit to before you can connect with divine spiritual purpose. This is often because God knows that if you don't understand how to submit to another person, you may never understand how to submit to Him. There are many people who never connect with divine destiny until they have understood how to serve someone else. Jesus came as God but knelt before John the Baptist and said, "You know what: before I start my ministry I must submit to the authority that was here before me."

Even though He as God created John the Baptist, He recognized John as the cutting edge of God's move and submitted to that move in order to project it into the next level or dimension in God. In a similar way, David was under the authority of his father. He wasn't old enough or counted worthy to go to the battlefront but he could lead a donkey to the battlefront with food for his brothers. He was simply a servant at heart. David went to the battlefield not to fight, but as a servant in submission to his father. You need to understand this mystery of God that while he was under the authority of his earthly father and in his errand of obedience he actually connected with the mission of his heavenly father.

I remember the testimony of a great man of God who explained how his pastor saved his life and ministry from pride. As a young man and part of this ministry, he had a gift of teaching and had become proud and so self-conscious that he often criticized others when they preached and felt his own gift was not well appreciated by the senior pastor. He thought they should give him more time to teach. But the senior pastor recognised his problem and instead of giving him the prominent position he sought, the pastor actually sent him to do menial tasks that infuriated him and for a while he said he hated his senior pastor. However later as he matured he realized what this spiritually mature man was doing and he blessed God for allowing him to be guided and disciplined by this man of God who loved him enough to discipline him. His pastor taught him humility otherwise God would have had to humble him.

David was ready to do anything to please God, he was ready to put his life on the line for the honour of God and so God honoured him. God taught David how to step forward boldly. Everyone tried to discourage him, especially his brothers, but God had taught him when no one was looking in the wilderness how to step forward. Therefore he stepped forward with God. He refused to be intimidated. He refused to be afraid. He refused the harassment of the enemy. Nothing could stop him from stepping forward. In the previous verses, God had anointed him secretly in his father's house. I believe that when David got to that place where performance was needed, he had a sense destiny. He knew that this was part of his destiny and while all the soldiers were quaking he stepped forward. I pray for you the grace to step forward in the moment of destiny in Jesus name. There are people as the bible says, who like the sons of Ephraim in the day of battle with bows and arrows turn back. I pray that you will not turn back in the day that God wants to make you. You will not turn back in your hour of victory in Jesus name.

One of the things God taught David was how to accept responsibility. Even Saul the king who was a head taller than everybody in Israel tried to discourage him. Saul was afraid for his life and his throne; they were more important to him than the honour of God and eventually he lost the things he put before the honour of God. David disregarded his life to defend the honour of God and not only did he find his life he received God's honour. Saul's crown and position had become an idol in his life, which led to his downfall.

God taught David how to step forward, he refused to be intimidated and to fear, he rejected the harassment of the enemy to stop him from going forward. When in chapter 16 of first Samuel he was anointed secretly in his father's house, he knew that God had chosen him to be king. He also had opportunity to prove the anointing and presence of God in his life when he encountered the lion and the bear while on assignment for his earthly father. He sensed in that moment in time that it was part of his destiny to fight and defeat Goliath and become the next king of Israel.

In Psalm 18, David describes dangers that had surrounded him that were physical, spiritual, social and emotional but in his distress he called upon the Lord. There is an amazing description of how David describes God rising up from heaven to help him. [Psalm 18:6-17] There is a pattern we can learn from David; he was anointed king as a teenager but did not enter the promise of God for many years. Saul became jealous and hunted him, gave his wife to another man and for several years David ran from the wrath and irrationality of Saul to the extent that he sought shelter with the enemies of Israel in Gath. Incredulous, this was where Goliath came from. It is really sad when a man becomes safer in the hands of his enemies than with his family and friends. David found favour with a Philistine warlord called Achish and settled in Ziglag for one year and four months.

In 1 Samuel 29-30 a time came and the Philistines were going to fight Israel and Achish took David and his men along. As soon as the other Philistines saw them they called Achish and challenged him about the loyalty of David and if David would be willing to kill his country-men. This prompted Achish to ask David and his men to return to Ziglag. When they returned, they found Ziglag had been ransacked and all their wives and children captured.
This was perhaps one of the great defining moments in David's life, he could have moaned and complained, he could have

done any number of things but he did not. The Bible says that he pressed into God in worshipful inquiry; he did not challenge God rather, he encouraged himself in the Lord. He sought for strength from God and even in his distress he was sensible enough to ask God for counsel.

He knew that there is always a strategy with God that God is willing to release. If we will ask God nicely, not in panic, but in boldness and confidence He will surely answer us. If you can trust God in your moment of greatest need you will align yourself for the greatest of blessings.

David accepted responsibility to lead by faith - observe that his faith was based on what God said he should do. Consider the challenge that David faced at this point in time, his men were talking of stoning him! But David kept a cool mind and dedicated trust in God. If you will trust God, and allow God to work through you, he will guide you into a new level of breakthrough. Today, people breakdown easily because they have not been taught how to turn to God and persevere and fight for their spiritual inheritance.

We must try to listen and receive God's strategy for our circumstances and move forward confidently so that God can fulfill His promises concerning us. You must hear and understand and have confidence in God's strategy for you. Moses had a strategy, Joshua had a strategy, and Gideon was told what to do. Making enquiries and receiving God's point of view became a pattern throughout David's life.

We must learn to listen and obey to be victorious warriors. Jesus healed the sick in so many ways; He was always listening to the Father for the strategy of the hour. Every challenge is part of God's plan to bring you into your inheritance, never give up, you are destined to move forward.

1 Timothy 1:18-19 encourages us to fight for our prophetic destiny. God had anointed David king but here he was at Ziglag and it appeared he had lost everything. God was watching to know if David was willing to believe Him and fight for his prophetic inheritance.

Sometimes we can miss God's purpose because we don't understand God's timing and so we give up too soon. Although David was anointed as a 17 year old he did not ascend the throne till he was about 30 but he did not give up, he kept pressing until he entered the rest of God that had been declared concerning him.

The Warrior's secret code:
Continue to declare the prophetic word in your life
Pray in the Holy Spirit
Resist anyone or anything that will weaken your faith
Maintain a constant spirit of praise and worship

Has God been speaking to you about stepping forward? About doing something in the house of God and for the kingdom of God? Perhaps, it is about stepping forward at work but you have been passive, content with flowing with the tide. Today, I declare in the name of Jesus Christ that you should move forward, break off every fear and intimidation, and step out to possess your possession. Heaven is waiting, hell is watching. Are you going to be passive or are you going to press forward into battle? The victory is already yours so go get it in Jesus name.

Responsibility is the only thing that releases God's ability in you. There is ability in you beyond what you can ask or imagine and beyond what you know. It is as you take on responsibility that the anointing of God is released to you.

The anointing you don't use will never be replenished and will never be multiplied and will never grow. And sometimes you don't even know what is inside you because you are not the one who put it there. It is only as God brings opportunity your way that you can exercise responsibility. God sometimes will disguise certain circumstances as work or trial. Don't run from it rather step forward. God never called an idle person. Everyone that God called was already busy. The busier you are, the more God will want to use you. If you are not doing something already I'm not sure God is likely to find you useful.

Today I want to prophesy and declare to you "It is time to move forward. You are destined to move forward. You are destined to enter your destiny in God. God has not given you the spirit of fear but of love, power and of a sound mind. Therefore today, I uproot every symptom of fear, procrastination and passivity in your life. I declare that from today you begin to enjoy what God has prepared for you in Jesus name. God said, "I have set a table before you in the presence of your enemies." There will always be challenges and enemies but He said, "I have set a table and I'm with you to make sure you eat off the table untill your cup is overflowing. I will serve you at that table and make your cup overflow." Only God can serve our cup and make it overflow. He said, "But you must get to that table first. Take the next step. Move forward. Get to that table. It's prepared for you. Don't be intimidated. Don't be afraid. Step forward. I'm with you." It's time to possess your possession. Heaven is waiting for you to step forward. You are born to triumph.

WARRIORS REFUSE TO FEAR

> *"For we do not wrestle against flesh and blood, but against principalities, against powers, against the rulers of the darkness of this age, against spiritual hosts of wickedness in the heavenly places."*
> *Ephesians 6:12 NKJV*

Our battles are essentially spiritual and it takes a spiritual approach to have complete victory over the issues of life. The root of victory is faith and the root of failure is fear. The effects of fear are very visible, they include discouragement, depression, confusion, hopelessness - this makes many Christians unable to fulfill their destiny because the spirit of fear actually stops you from releasing your gifts and talents.

It is important to recognise that you already have a position of authority in God.

> "He who dwells in the secret place of the Most High Shall abide under the shadow of the Almighty. I will say of the LORD, "He is my refuge and my fortress; My God, in Him I will trust."
> Psalm 91:1-2 NKJV

> "My foot stands in an even place; In the congregations I will bless the LORD."
> Psalm 26:12 NKJV

> "And you He made alive, who were dead in trespasses and sins, in which you once walked according to the course of this world, according to the prince of the power of the air, the spirit who now works in the sons of disobedience,"
> Ephesians 2:1-2 NKJV

> "And raised us up together, and made us sit together in the heavenly places in Christ Jesus,"
> Ephesians 2:6 NKJV

Satan's task is to try and knock you out of position so he can use the authority you already have against you. If you don't walk in your God given authority, someone will take it and use it against you. Fear is the basic way the enemy uses to take your authority from you.

Fear will change your focus; it will make you focus on yourself and as soon as you become preoccupied with yourself, either with your strength or weakness you will start to loose the focus you should keep on Jesus the author and finisher of your faith. Love is what helps you retain your focus on God and others and deny self.

> *"There is no fear in love; but perfect love casts out fear, because fear involves torment. But he who fears has not been made perfect in love."*
> *1 John 4:18 NKJV*

Whenever you embrace fear it will knock you out of your spiritual position and make you loose spiritual effectiveness. Many people will fight the effects of this spirit all their life but until the root is dealt with, they will settle for less than God's will. If you examine closely the incident in the Garden of Eden, we see that the tactics of the enemy was to displace Adam and Eve in order to take authority that belonged to them. He has not changed in his tactics. The major way Satan makes people to loose spiritual authority and position is disobedience and sin.

> *"And Jesus came and spoke to them, saying, "All authority has been given to Me in heaven and on earth. Go therefore and make disciples of all the nations, baptizing them in the name of the Father and of the Son and of the Holy Spirit, "teaching them to observe all things that I have commanded you; and lo, I am with you always, even to the end of the age." Amen"*
> *Matthew 28:18-20 NKJV*

> *""Behold, I give you the authority to trample on serpents and scorpions, and over all the power of the enemy, and nothing shall by any means hurt you."*
> *Luke 10:19 NKJV*

What we now have through Jesus Christ is more than what Satan stole from Adam and Eve. Adam only had dominion on earth but Jesus has now given us dominion in heaven and on earth. Therefore, in the spirit realm, a believer in Christ has more authority and a position that is above the devil.

> *"Neither give place to the devil."*
> *Ephesians 4:27 NKJV*

Satan will try to steal your authority by bringing sin into your life even when you are determined to serve God, he will try to knock you out of position through fear and intimidation. This is why it is important to confront your heart from time to time and examine where you are in your worship and devotion to Christ.

> *"That I may know Him and the power of His resurrection, and the fellowship of His sufferings, being conformed to His death, if, by any means, I may attain to the resurrection from the dead. Not that I have already attained, or am already perfected; but I press on, that I may lay hold of that for which Christ Jesus has also laid hold of me. Brethren, I do not count myself to have apprehended; but one thing I do, forgetting those things which are behind and reaching forward to those things which are ahead, I press toward the goal for the prize of the upward call of God in Christ Jesus."*
> *Philippians 3:10-14 NKJV*

The highest goal of the Christian is to know Him and develop a godly character. It is possible to pursue power and go from one anointing service to the other but be unwilling to confront and deal with the anger, unforgiveness and bitterness in our own heart.

The church is the body of Christ and every believer has a function in that body and a gift to function with. But except you walk in and exercise your authority the enemy will use your gift against you.

> *"Therefore I remind you to stir up the gift of God which is in you through the laying on of my hands. For God has not given us a spirit*

of fear, but of power and of love and of a sound mind."
2 Timothy 1:6-7 NKJV

Your gift needs to be stirred up by exercise, you are to steward it diligently. If you don't stir it up and engage it, the enemy will intimidate you. Many believers are ineffective because their gifts have become dormant.

"For the gifts and the calling of God are irrevocable."
Romans 11:29 NKJV

"As each one has received a gift, minister it to one another, as good stewards of the manifold grace of God."
1 Peter 4:10 NKJV

A Christian will begin to backslide when he or she does not function in their gift or calling. An idle believer is soon isolated and becomes an easy prey for the enemy. When David refused to go to war, he became subject to temptation that almost derailed him from God's purpose and anointing on his life.

"And it came to pass, after the year was expired, at the time when kings go forth to battle, that David sent Joab, and his servants with him, and all Israel; and they destroyed the children of Ammon, and besieged Rabbah. But David tarried still at Jerusalem."
2 Samuel 11:1 NKJV

Your authority and position is to steward the manifold grace of God and so every believer has gifts and talents but if these remain unused, fear, timidity and intimidation becomes the consequence of inactivity.

Intimidation simply means to inspire someone with fear, to discourage or suppress, to make timid. The main objective of the enemy is to stop you from action, to paralyse you from moving forward and force you into submission by putting you under fear and a feeling of inadequacy. Once you retreat out of fear, you become a slave to this spirit and the gift of God and ability of God inside you can no longer function properly.

> *"For though we walk in the flesh, we do not war according to the flesh. For the weapons of our warfare are not carnal but mighty in God for pulling down strongholds, casting down arguments and every high thing that exalts itself against the knowledge of God, bringing every thought into captivity to the obedience of Christ,"*
> 2Corinthians 10:3-5 NKJV

Satan is the originator of fear. He attacks through our thoughts, imaginations, or circumstances and through other people who are already under his influence. His objective is to control and limit us. Warriors refuse to fear and be intimidated because their minds are stayed on God's word.

Under the influence of fear, there is confusion, frustration, and discouragement. People will lose proper perspective; everything will look so difficult and impossible. Your focus shifts from God to yourself until you feel ineffective, useless or worthless. This happened to God's prophet Elijah in 1 Kings 17-19.

When Elijah did not confront Jezebel, he was knocked out of his position of authority, so his gift became dormant and ineffective. He went in a wrong direction. God had to challenge him in 1 Kings 19:9 "What are you doing here?" You need to ask yourself today, how much of where you are now is a consequence of what you are running away from?

In 1 Kings 19:15-17, As soon as Elijah was knocked out of position by fear, God instructed him to anoint someone else to replace him. Fear stopped him from completing his assignment. Don't allow fear to paralyse you. Whatever you fear, you have decided to honour more than God. Fear is a spirit and must be addressed in the spirit realm.

You have been given the spirit of power, love and a sound mind. In 2 Kings 9:30-37 Jehu who was anointed king over Israel refused to submit his authority to Jezebel, he confronted her and destroyed her.

> *"Now it happened, when Joram saw Jehu, that he said, "Is it peace, Jehu?" So he answered, "What peace, as long as the harlotries of your mother Jezebel and her witchcraft are so many?"*
> *2 Kings 9:22 NKJV*

Jehu recognised that fear is a function of the spirit of witchcraft - witchcraft is exercised when someone seeks to control another by fear or intimidation. Jezebel had such a strong controlling and intimidating spirit that her husband and entire nation gave way to her. When you submit to fear, you loose peace, confidence, courage and endurance.

Whatever you don't confront will not change. If evil is ignored it only becomes stronger. Our major weapon of victory is the Word of God.

The major purpose of the spirit of fear is to make us give up our authority and this renders our gifts useless. When fear grips you, you become reduced to operating in your limited strength and ability without God's ability. This puts you into a defensive rather than an offensive position and our most vulnerable position is when we are retreating.

The question is, how can a fearful person appropriate boldness? Boldness is a function of power, love and a sound mind [2 Timothy 1:6-7]. True boldness comes from God and is fuelled by righteous living. Only a boldness given life by a godly character will awaken the gifts in us. There are some people who don't have virtue behind their boldness so their strength is superficial. The bold face only becomes a mask for arrogance or ignorance, their roots are shallow and a strong storm will expose them.

God alone and His word and promises are sufficient as the source of our confidence.

> *"The LORD is my light and my salvation; Whom shall I fear? The LORD is the strength of my life; Of whom shall I be afraid?*
> *Psalm 27:1 NKJV*

David is a very good example of someone who knew the power of God and his boldness in God enabled him to fulfill his destiny when he marched forward to fight Goliath. It was a situation where the whole nation was intimidated but David boldly made a confrontational statement. It was based on confidence in God. The older brothers felt naked as he exposed their own fears. When David's boldness exposed their weakness, they tried to intimidate him. In this same way Jesus constantly faced attacks of intimidation by lawyers and the Pharisees.

David boldly declared the faithfulness of God. The men of Israel had only seen how big Goliath was but David only saw the faithfulness of God. David's boldness brought out the gift of God (ability) and he defeated Goliath.

Our New Covenant with God is a Covenant of Power [2

Corinthians 3:7-8; Hebrews 13:5-6]

You will find boldness in believers who do not trust in their own strength alone because people or circumstances or the devil does not intimidate them. Their God cannot be intimidated and they believe absolutely that God is with them. This level of confidence is available to every believer in Christ.

> *"Behold, I give you the authority to trample on serpents and scorpions, and over all the power of the enemy, and nothing shall by any means hurt you."*
> Luke 10:19 NKJV

Does your confidence rest in what God has said or in what you see and experience? Do you base your faith on what has happened to others? If you measure things by your past, you will never grow beyond it. Jesus has given us all power and authority over all the power of the enemy. Please believe Him. The root of fear is self-preservation.

This is what Jesus had to say:

> *"He who finds his life will lose it, and he who loses his life for My sake will find it."*
> Matthew 10:39 NKJV

> *"For whoever desires to save his life will lose it, but whoever loses his life for My sake and the gospel's will save it."*
> Mark 8:35 NKJV

Peter was bold, strong willed and a fearless man, yet he denied Christ. This should warn us that freedom from fear is not the result of a strong personality or a bold face. It is the function of an active faith. Peter was not a coward; he single handedly confronted a mob of soldiers yet a small girl intimidated him. [John 18:3,10; Matthew 26:69-70]

We must keep examining our heart. The motive for Peter's boldness was possibly pride and not the love of God; the disciples were all looking for power and position. This was why when it was time to pray and draw on the strength of God, he protected what he thought was his strength by sleeping. [Matthew 26:31-35; Luke 22:21-24] But true strength is in the spirit unseen realm accessed by prayer and communion with God. Wherever the love of self overrides a man, it will give birth to the root of fear.

> *"Love has been perfected among us in this: that we may have boldness in the Day of Judgment; because as He is, so are we in this world. There is no fear in love; but perfect love casts out fear, because fear involves torment. But he who fears has not been made perfect in love.*
> *1 John 4:17-18 NKJV*

Only perfect love casts out fear and gives us boldness.

> *"And they overcame him by the blood of the Lamb and by the word of their testimony, and they did not love their lives to the death."*
> *Revelation 12:11 NKJV*

Fear and intimidation is magnified when we focus on ourselves and not on the ability of God. Do you remember the three Hebrew boys? Their focus was keenly on God.

> *"Shadrach, Meshach, and Abed-Nego answered and said to the king, "O Nebuchadnezzar, we have no need to answer you in this matter. If that is the case, our God whom we serve is able to deliver us from the burning fiery furnace, and He will deliver us from your*

hand, O king. "But if not, let it be known to you, O king, that we do not serve your gods, nor will we worship the gold image which you have set up."
Daniel 3:16-18 NKJV

Fear should never torment a child of God if you have truly laid down your life out of love for Jesus Christ. We must understand that not all boldness is motivated by love. It seems to me that some part of Peter's boldness might have been motivated by approval of others because as soon as there was no one there to impress, a small girl put him to shame.

But after the Holy Ghost came upon the disciples, they became bold and their love for Jesus could not be suppressed. If you truly love Jesus, you will refuse to bow to the spirit of fear. The dangerous thing is that we tend to serve whatever we fear and we have a choice to fear men or to fear God. If you choose to fear God, you will not need to serve the whims of men.

The Bible talks a lot about the FEAR OF GOD. [Isaiah 11:3; Proverbs 1:7; Proverbs 2:5; Proverbs 9:10; 2 Corinthians 7:1; Hebrews 12:14]

The only way to be free from the spirit of fear is to walk in the fear of God. We need strong confidence to develop boldness to go God's way rather than the ways of man. [Proverbs 14:26]

A Warriors delights in the fear of God

The fear of God is giving God the place of glory, honour, reverence, thanksgiving and praise that He deserves in our lives. God only truly occupies that place of honour in our lives when we put His will and desires above our own.

> *"The fear of man brings a snare, But whoever trusts in the LORD shall be safe."*
> *Proverbs 29:25 NKJV*

The fear of man will put you in anxiety, dread and suspicion. When gripped by the fear of man, you are constantly hiding from harm and shame, trying to avoid rejection and confrontation. We become so busy trying to protect ourselves that we become ineffective at serving God. It is the fear of man that enables Satan to steal your God given authority and demobilize your gift. When we please men in order to escape reproach we deny God. You will serve and obey whom you fear but you cannot serve two masters. [Isaiah 51:7-13; Galatians 1:10]

The Warrior understand that the love of God is the cure for fear

If you truly love God, you will fear Him and His fear will swallow up the lesser fears. When we treat God as familiar we lose perspective of His proper place. Let me ask you, what is your behavior before and during the worship of God? Do you know that lack of respect for servants of God is a lack of respect for God? What do you do when someone is leading worship or standing behind the pulpit to minister? Are you generally reverent around the things of God? Sometimes your general attitude, reverence and disposition say a lot about your readiness to succeed with God. [Acts 5:5; Leviticus 10:1-3]

The fear and love of God will draw you into intimacy with God. When you are captured by the fear of men, you will feel more comfortable in the presence of men than you would in the presence of God. A person is seduced into sin when he takes as common what God counts as holy. [Hebrews 10:26-31]

Do you know that when God called Moses up the mountain, he actually called for Aaron to come along with him? Yes, Moses and Aaron were invited but only Moses responded. When you refuse God's invitation, you will respond to the degrading invitations of men as Aaron did. [Exodus 19:24; Exodus 32:1; Exodus 32:35]

This is in clear contrast to Joshua who was not formally invited but who had such a heart for God that he went up half way uninvited and avoided the idolatry in the camp. This provoked God to promote him. It was his heart for God that led to his exalted position as the one to take over from Moses. [Exodus 32:17; 33:11]

God has given us a spirit of a sound mind, a sound mind knows what God is saying and doing per time, nothing brings fear like ignorance. Only knowledge gives us strength to escape the spirit of fear but what kind of knowledge should we seek? [Proverbs 24:5; Proverbs 11:9]

The spirit of a sound mind is not the product of natural wisdom or Bible school training; it is the product of knowing the mind of Christ by revelation knowledge. It's not enough to know chapter and verse in the Bible; we must also receive the spirit and the power into our hearts. When a sound mind is formed in you, you speak with boldness and authority. [Acts 4:13; Acts 6:10; 2 Corinthians 3:6; Ephesians 1:17-19; Ephesians 3:16-19; Colossians 1:9-11]

Strength is a function of revealed knowledge by God. Revealed knowledge comes from the pursuit of intimacy with God through the Holy Spirit. It is by understanding the truth of God's word and your redemption by the blood of Jesus that you will fulfill all your potential as a warrior. [Matthew 7:28-29; John 5:19,30; John 7:16; John 12:49; Joshua 1:7-8; Philippians 1:27-28]

Postscript

MARCH FORWARD IN FAITH LIKE THE WARRIOR YOU ARE

Life demands that we contest to conquer. It is part of God's divine programme for man to have opposition and challenges, but every obstacle is meant to become a miracle and every challenge a stepping-stone to upward change. No challenge or discouragement is strong enough to discourage us from following the plans of God. [Romans 8:37 Mark 5:25-34; Mark 10:46-52] Challenges are part of the arrangement if you are to possess your inheritance. God will not cut corners in your assignment. If you see no challenges you will see no victory. Every challenge targets your confidence and when confidence suffers, courage is lost. Without courage you cannot possess your inheritance. Cheer up and brace up, the fight is not over until you win.

There are things you must know about challenges; every challenge and opposition is initiated and planned by the devil. He may use people, believers or unbelievers and he may use circumstances like hunger or hardship. This is why you must never take things to heart and hate people; rather you must learn how to face the main culprit. Your fight is never about the people but the enemy behind it all. Don't react to the challenge in the flesh but in the spirit. Don't ever see your challenge as an affliction, don't feel depressed or dejected, see it as a sign of impending promotion because Satan is not bothered if you are already a failure. Challenges and oppositions are a sign that your star is rising.

Every opposition is a tool of distraction. Don't yield to it. Distraction is what makes you major on minor issues. Every challenge is meant to distract you. If the enemy cannot derail you he tries to delay you with distractions. If your focus is steered off course long enough it could become your destination. It is important to fight fear as you would fight sin and death. Be not afraid. Fear is the foothold of Satan in any life. The blind beggar Batimaeus and the woman with issue of blood overcame their fear before they could release their faith and receive their healing from Jesus.

Fear breeds confusion and instability, it often works with the spirit of poverty and sickness. The spirit of poverty says God is not able to handle what is ahead for me; fear also works with sickness to weaken your ability to stand. Fear will work with anger so that you react in anger instead of embracing change. Fear is a very powerful but unpleasant feeling associated with risks or danger and this emotion can be real or imagined. Biologically, it is a defensive response to a stimulus that has entered the atmosphere around us. However, most of your fears are often based on something you think may happen in the future. When you begin to allow your mind create a scenario that is not based on what God has said, it creates friction and vexation in your soul. This may result in weakness or infirmity. God's commandment to Joshua stressed courage as a key requirement because there is no promised land without giants. Our nature as Christians must be boldness. But boldness must be stirred up and only knowledge can stir up our boldness. The consciousness of your right standing with God is what will instill boldness and courage in you. [Romans 8:31; Colossians 1:9-13; Ephesians 3:16-20; Isaiah 54:11-17]

Each time the enemy reminds you of past mistakes, and you dwell on them, you lose strength, he wants you to feel unworthy but cheer up God is not holding your faults against you. To remain bold you must always remind yourself of the love of God. [Jude 20-22] But also it is important to constantly conduct self-examination because self-examination is full proof of Christian maturity. You must be ready to stand in the place of personal examination.

Examine yourself frequently and ensure you know where you are going because if you don't know where to go, challenges and circumstances of life have a way of dictating and showing you where to go. You must have a life vision that dictates both the momentum and direction of your life. There must be something you are living for. If you don't know what to live for you won't know what to run from. It is your life's vision that gives you great motivation and energizes you towards success and to overcome challenges. It is a product of the mind and imagination. Until your mind and imagination can fashion a great tomorrow you may not get there. The advantage for a believer is that through a purified imagination you can project into the future and receive God's counsel for your life. [Genesis 13:14-15; Genesis 15:5-6]

God stimulated Abraham's imagination with illustrations so that he had a continuous focus on God's promise through his imagination despite his personal challenges.

There is great power in imagination and your imagination will play a pivotal role in overcoming challenges and guiding you into entering the destiny of greatness that God has prepared for you. Imagination has the ability to draw towards you the things you imagine.

Imagination creates a vision and expectation - expectation generates enthusiasm, enthusiasm always dismantles opposition and challenges through strategic activity.

As a believer who is wholesome in the spirit of your mind, sometimes God will take over your imagination so that the Holy Spirit can think through you. As you grow in the Lord, you may initiate the thinking but as you meditate with God, He begins to plant His ideas and programmes into your mind. Personal responsibility is therefore required to cultivate solitude and clarify what The Lord is saying. Many things will seek your attention but only one thing is needful, your vision or assignment. How bright you can keep your vision will determine the speed of your accomplishment.

Keep on at your job, pursuit, vision - whatever you are doing is going to affect the devil, so do more. Remember also that in the kingdom of God, nothing works without love. Satan may use people to provoke you to hatred and bitterness but your depth of love determines your height in life. Be determined to be a repairer not a destroyer, we are to be builders of the body not bulldozers. True love involves sacrifice, no matter what anyone does to abuse or humiliate you, you must work towards the highest good of others and you will continue to enjoy favour with God. [Galatians 5:6; Matthew 5:11]

As a warrior of righteousness you must realize that behind every opposition is a spiritual storm, address it as Jesus did in the boat. When Jesus addressed the storm as an evil thing, it obeyed Him. When you sense opposition act boldly in the scriptures against Satan. Be quick to launch a counter attack in the spirit. [Matthew 8:26; Hebrews 12:12-15]

You must believe God for signs and wonders; expect a miracle as God's seal of approval. When challenges and opposition rise up against you make sure you continue to progress until your progress silences the protest of challengers.

Confession

Zechariah 2:5
"For I,' says the LORD, 'will be a wall of fire all around her, and I will be the glory in her midst."

The Lord Jesus will be a wall of fire providing protection against the enemies of my life, as the hills surround Jerusalem so shall The Lord of hosts will defend me. The Lord of Hosts will be a wall of fire around my life, my family, ministry and my city. The Lord shall also be the glory in the midst of my affairs, the out flowing of the radiance of JEHOVAH's glory, the splendour that filled the tabernacle of Moses, that flooded Solomon's temple, the same shekinah glory will preserve my life from the enemy. The very presence of The Lord who says I will never leave you nor forsake you will rise up to defend me. The glory of God will separate me, insulate me and terminate every enemy advances against me. Jesus is my security and no man shall put me down. Christ has obtained eternal redemption for me and I am accepted and forgiven. Jesus will never let me down. I praise Him for His steadfast protection over me and all that is mine. The Lord will establish peace in my borders; the comfort that is the expression of His out flowing nature of peace shall reside in my heart. The Lord of peace will give me His peace personally and always and in every way. The Blessed God and Father of our Lord Jesus Christ the Father of mercies and God of all comfort will ensure that I am never short of mercy and comfort. I receive unlimited supply of grace and favour. This year, Jesus will breathe His peace with authority and power into every troubled situation in my life and that of my family. God will bring unity and divine reconciliation into every conflict that has troubled my life. Jesus will stand tall with me this year and the resources of His Mighty Name will answer to me. I receive calmness, wholeness and harmony in my life in Jesus name.

Isaiah 28:16
> "Therefore thus says the Lord GOD: "Behold, I lay in Zion a stone for a foundation, A tried stone, a precious cornerstone, a sure foundation; Whoever believes will not act hastily."

JEHOVAH is my sure foundation, The Lord who brought me out of a horrible pit and the miry clay of sin has set my feet upon a rock and established my steps and my goings. My life and destiny shall be built on the sure foundation that will make me shine and do exploits; He who began a good work in me will complete it until the day of Jesus Christ. In the name of Jesus Christ my life will find solid ground and stability The Lord will give me a steadfast heart, which no unworthy affection may drag down and an unconquerable heart that no tribulation can wear out, He will give me an upright heart which no unworthy purpose can tempt aside, and impart to me today, the understanding to know Him, diligence to seek Him, wisdom to find Him and faithfulness to embrace Him to the end.

JEHOVAH MEKADDISHKEM will sanctify me and bring significant spiritual growth into my life this year. He will refine my character and purify my life. The Lord will cleanse me from secret faults and protect me from secret sins. Good health is one of life's priceless blessings, The Lord who heals

JEHOVAH RAPHA will guard me from sickness and illness, His divine presence as The Lord who heals will shield me and my family from every present evil, The Lord will not only heal and prevent sickness, He will sustain my health, He will guide me into health and I will not be disappointed. I will never drink polluted waters of bitterness or despair because The Lord my healer will help me and sustain me. The balm in Gilead will soothe me, the fountain of living waters will satisfy me, the God of all comfort will comfort me, the life giving Spirit will quicken me, the sweet ointment poured forth will make my life a fragrance of life to all that meet me.

Isaiah 9:2
"The people who walked in darkness Have seen a great light; Those who dwelt in the land of the shadow of death, Upon them a light has shined."

In the light of Jesus today I will see light, I will arise and shine for the light of His glory has come to shine on me and lead me out of darkness, The Lord God will not leave me without a witness of divine guidance. He shall be a lamp to my feet and a light to my path. God will reveal to me His very best. In Him there is no shadow of turning. He will multiply and increase my joy and bring a glorious harvest into my life. I receive divine assistance and live in dominion over all the powers of darkness; the quickening power of the Holy Spirit revitalises my soul and gives life and strength into my physical body. Whatever is robbing me of life and energy whether spiritually, physically or materially is uprooted in Jesus name. The Lord will use me for whatever purpose He requires, the Lord will quicken me in those moments when the spirit is willing and the flesh is weak. I ask the Lord to breathe freshness and newness of life into me today. I pray that this year the ever-present Jesus will be my supervisor. The Lord will give me capacity and ability to perceive or see from divine perspectives and see things through the eyes of Jesus. I pray that today I will rely on and depend on the supervision of Jesus in my life this year; He will be the author and finisher of my faith.

Christ will help me towards excellence, if the ministration in the Old Testament was such that Moses' face was set aglow how much more shall my life move from glory to glory and radiate the majesty and brightness of the King of kings. God will work in me to mature me and prepare me for His divine blessings therefore, I shall walk in excellence of spirit. I come against every sense of mediocrity in my life. God's spirit of excellence shall overflow around me in Jesus name. The Mighty Counselor will counsel me in wonderful things; He will bring insight of heavenly origin into human difficulties through me and make me a marvel to the world. Amen.

www.ingramcontent.com/pod-product-compliance
Lightning Source LLC
Chambersburg PA
CBHW061446040426
42450CB00007B/1231